PHILIP ALLAN

LITERATURE GUIDE

FOR A-LEVEL

THE GREAT GATSBY
F. SCOTT FITZGERALD

Anne Crow

Series editor: Nicola Onyett

If you require help

Philip Allan Updates, an imprint of Hodder Education, an Hachette UK company, Market Place, Deddington, Oxfordshire OX15 0SE

Orders

Bookpoint Ltd, 130 Milton Park, Abingdon, Oxfordshire OX14 4SB

tel: 01235 827827

fax: 01235 400401

e-mail: education@bookpoint.co.uk

Lines are open 9.00 a.m.–5.00 p.m., Monday to Saturday, with a 24-hour message answering service. You can also order through the Philip Allan Updates website: www.philipallan.co.uk

© Philip Allan Updates 2010

ISBN 978-1-4441-1621-2

First printed 2010

Impression number 5 4

Year 2014

Printed in Spain

Hachette UK's policy is to use papers that are natural, renewable and recyclable products and made from wood grown in sustainable forests. The logging and manufacturing processes are expected to conform to the environmental regulations of the country of origin.

Cover photo: Robert Redford as Jay Gatsby in the 1974 film. © Photos 12/Alamy

Contents

Using this guide

Why read this guide?

The purposes of this A-level Literature Guide are to enable you to organise your thoughts and responses to the text, deepen your understanding of key features and aspects and help you to address the particular requirements of examination questions and coursework tasks in order to obtain the best possible grade. It will also prove useful to those of you writing a coursework piece on the text as it provides a number of summaries, lists, analyses and references to help with the content and construction of the assignment.

Note that teachers and examiners are seeking above all else evidence of an *informed personal response to the text*. A guide such as this can help you to understand the text and form your own opinions, and it can suggest areas to think about, but it cannot replace your own ideas and responses as an informed and autonomous reader.

Page references in this guide refer to the 1990 Penguin Classics edition of the text, edited by Tony Tanner.

How to make the most of this guide

You may find it useful to read sections of this guide when you need them, rather than reading it from start to finish. For example, you may find it helpful to read the *Contexts* section before you start reading the text, or to read the *Chapter summaries and commentaries* section in conjunction with the text — whether to back up your first reading of it at school or college or to help you revise. The sections relating to the Assessment Objectives will be especially useful in the weeks leading up to the exam.

Key elements

Look at the **Context** boxes to find interesting facts that are relevant to the text.

Context

Be exam-ready

Broaden your thinking about the text by answering the questions in the **Pause for thought** boxes. These help you to consider your own opinions in order to develop your skills of criticism and analysis.

*Pause for **Thought*** **Ⅱ**

Build critical skills

Taking it further boxes suggest poems, films, etc. that provide further background or illuminating parallels to the text.

Taking it **Further** ▶

Where to find out more

Use the **Task boxes** to develop your understanding of the text and test your knowledge of it. Answers for some of the tasks are given online, and do not forget to look online for further self-tests on the text.

Task

Test yourself

Follow up cross references to the **Top ten quotations** (see pp. 90–92), where each quotation is accompanied by a commentary that shows why it is important.

❮ Top ten *quotation*

Know your text

Don't forget to go online: **www.philipallan.co.uk/literatureguidesonline** where you can find masses of additional resources **free**, including interactive questions, podcasts, exam answers and a glossary.

Synopsis

Nick Carraway introduces himself at the beginning of the novel. He fought in the First World War, and this made him restlessly unwilling to work in the family business, so he moved to New York in the summer of 1922. He rented a cheap bungalow in the West Egg district of Long Island, a wealthy but unfashionable area populated by the newly rich. Nick's next-door neighbour in West Egg is a mysterious man named Jay Gatsby who lives in a huge, mock-French mansion and throws extravagant parties every Saturday night.

Unlike the other inhabitants of West Egg, Nick boasts a possible connection with the English aristocracy, was educated at Yale University and has social connections in East Egg, the fashionable area of Long Island where the established upper classes live. One evening, Nick drives out to East Egg for dinner with his cousin, Daisy Buchanan and her husband, Tom, whom Nick had known at Yale. Daisy and Tom introduce Nick to Jordan Baker, a beautiful, cynical, young professional golfer. Nick learns that Tom has a lover.

Soon after this Tom takes Nick to meet Myrtle Wilson, the wife of the garage mechanic in the valley of ashes, a grey industrial dumping ground between East and West Egg and Manhattan. Nick travels to the city with Tom and Myrtle, and, at a vulgar party in their apartment, Myrtle taunts Tom about Daisy. Tom breaks her nose, and Nick leaves hurriedly with Mr McKee, an effeminate neighbour.

Nick is invited to one of Gatsby's legendary parties. He meets Jordan; she introduces him to Gatsby, a young man with an irresistible smile who speaks with elaborate formality. It appears that he and Nick both served in the first division during the war, and they share a few vague reminiscences. Another day, Gatsby takes Nick to New York in his gorgeous car and gives him an extravagantly fictitious account of his life. In a speakeasy, he introduces Nick to Meyer Wolfshiem, the man who supposedly fixed the Baseball World Series in 1919.

After lunch, Nick meets Jordan, with whom he is now having a romantic relationship, and she tells him that Gatsby knew Daisy in Louisville in 1917 and is deeply in love with her. He spends many nights staring at the green light at the end of her dock, across the bay from his mansion, and his extravagant lifestyle and wild parties are an attempt to attract Daisy. Nick is overwhelmed by the splendour of Gatsby's dream. Jordan asks Nick to arrange a reunion between Gatsby and Daisy. Nick invites Daisy

Context

Francis Scott Fitzgerald and his wife, Zelda, lived in Great Neck, Long Island, while he was planning *The Great Gatsby*.

Context

America joined the First World War (the Great War) in April 1917.

to tea at his house, warning her not to bring Tom, but not telling her that Gatsby will be there. After an initially awkward meeting, Gatsby and Daisy revive their relationship and begin an affair.

Soon, Tom grows suspicious of his wife's relationship with Gatsby. At a luncheon at the Buchanans' house, Daisy behaves indiscreetly and Tom realises they are in love. Although Tom is himself involved in an extramarital affair, he is outraged. Daisy suggests that they go to town and Tom demands to drive Gatsby's car. Daisy chooses to travel with Gatsby in Tom's car. Tom stops in the valley of ashes for petrol, and Myrtle sees him from the garage window.

In the searing heat in a suite at the Plaza Hotel, music reminds Daisy of her romantic wedding day. Tom confronts Gatsby, revealing what he knows about Gatsby's lies and criminal activities. Shaken by these revelations, when both men try to force her to declare that she loves only them, Daisy withdraws into herself and begs Tom to take her home. Tom triumphantly sends her back to East Egg with Gatsby, attempting to prove that Gatsby cannot hurt him.

When Nick, Jordan, and Tom drive through the valley of ashes, they discover that Gatsby's car had struck and killed Myrtle after she had run out into the road. They rush back to East Egg, where Nick learns from Gatsby that Daisy was driving the car, but that Gatsby intends to take the blame. The next day, Tom tells Myrtle's husband, George, that Gatsby was the driver of the car. By the time Nick reaches Gatsby's mansion, Gatsby is dead. He seems to have been shot as he lay on an air-bed in the swimming pool. The discovery of Wilson's body leads to the conclusion that Wilson shot Gatsby and then turned the gun on himself.

The inquest comes to the obvious conclusion 'in order that the case might remain in its simplest form'. Nick arranges Gatsby's funeral, ends his relationship with Jordan, and moves back to the Midwest. Nick visits Gatsby's house one last time and experiences a moment of vision. Ever since the first settlers arrived on 'the fresh green breast of the new world', Americans have always had dreams which are doomed to be unachievable, and so Gatsby comes to stand for America itself.

Gatsby comes to stand for America itself

Commentary: **Nick comments that Tom had 'tanked up' at luncheon and was forcing Nick to accompany him. 'The supercilious assumption' (p. 27) was that Nick had nothing better to do. The slang term implies that Tom had consumed a large quantity of alcohol and compares him with a car; both Tom and a car have a large capacity and are very powerful. Using slang suggests contempt from the sober Nick, and his subsequent Latinate polysyllabic phrase 'supercilious assumption' both mocks Tom's heavy-handedness and conveys Nick's resentment.**

The valley of ashes was Fitzgerald's name for the area around Flushing Creek that had been acquired by the Brooklyn Ash Removal Company, which turned the salt marshes into a landfill site for garbage from the city and ashes from coal-burning furnaces. On one level it represents the grey, dismal environment of the Wilsons and the class to which they belong, ignored by the wealthy who pollute it. The valley is close to the lines of communication between the homes of the rich and the city, but the trains pass straight through, although forced to stop when barges are moving on the creek. Ironically, this 'dumping ground' is the inevitable end of the material possessions of the wealthy.

Fitzgerald calls the valley of ashes 'the waste land' (p. 27), which is the title of a poem by T. S. Eliot, published in 1922, three years before *The Great Gatsby*. Both writers present their readers with images of a barren landscape, where nothing grows. The valley of ashes seems to be watched over, but the eyes are not the eyes of God, just an abandoned advertisement, a symbol of materialism. Similarly, the Son of Man is neglected in Eliot's waste land, where there is only 'a heap of broken images', suggesting discarded idols. Both worlds are spiritually dead, and there is only 'fear in a handful of dust'. Fitzgerald sometimes refers to the ash as dust and it echoes God's words to Adam and Eve: 'Dust thou art and to dust thou shalt return.' However, neither writer seems to interpret this as a fear of death; it is rather a fear of a meaningless life.

Nick admires Myrtle's vitality, but he mocks her attempts to behave like a society hostess, calling her 'violently affected'. He mocks her movements because they lack natural grace and her voice that becomes mechanical with her efforts. It reveals much about Nick's values that he criticises her only for her working-class pretensions, not her immoral behaviour; he never mocks her for being unfaithful to her husband. She enters the

Context

Thomas Stearns Eliot (1888–1965) was a poet, critic and playwright, who was born in the United States but moved to England in 1914 and became a British subject in 1927. His most significant work is *The Waste Land* (1922), which expresses the disillusionment of the postwar generation with the hedonism of a materialistic society.

apartment block 'haughtily', has furnished it with French tapestried furniture, complains about the servants, acts bored and blasé, and affects 'an impressive hauteur'. However, there are some individual details that are quite touching in their naivety. Like a child on a birthday treat, she refuses to travel in an ordinary taxi. Her behaviour with the dog is childlike: she chooses one 'enthusiastically', strokes it 'with rapture', 'delicately' asks its gender, sends the elevator boy for a box of straw and some milk, kisses it 'with ecstasy', and then forgets about it, leaving it 'looking with blind eyes through the smoke and...groaning faintly'. The expensive dog-leash she buys and takes home symbolises Myrtle's position as a kept woman, and is, significantly, the means by which her husband finds out that she has a lover.

Nick's description of her as 'the despairing figure on the couch, bleeding fluently' (p. 39) sounds mocking; the adverb 'fluently' is usually associated with speech not blood, so he insensitively suggests that the fuss she is creating is out of all proportion to her wound. This image provides an ironic counterpoint to Jordan and Daisy in Chapter I, reclining languorously on their couches in their white dresses. Myrtle's image is not constructed to impress — she is real, a scarlet woman. Whereas Tom bruises Daisy's little finger without meaning to, he deliberately hits Myrtle so hard that he breaks her nose. She went home with 'her face bruised and her nose swollen' (p. 149), but the absence of a dressing suggests that Tom did not take her to hospital.

Chapter III

At one of Gatsby's parties, Nick listens to the rumours about his host before eventually meeting him and realising that they served in the same division during the Great War. Gatsby has a private conversation with Jordan, who tells Nick that Gatsby has told her something amazing. Nick glosses over the next few weeks, describing his routine, admitting that he was growing to like New York and getting closer to Jordan.

Commentary: **At Gatsby's party, the gaiety of West Egg is described as 'spectroscopic', so characterised by light, colour and energy, whereas the people who live in East Egg are conscious of their 'staid nobility' and are on their guard against any temptation to enjoy themselves. However, even they let down their guard and**

> *Pause for **Thought***
>
> When Nick arrived in Fifth Avenue he thought it looked 'almost pastoral' and he 'wouldn't have been surprised to see a great flock of white sheep'. What does this tell us about Nick?

> ...the gaiety of West Egg is 'spectroscopic'

break down under the influence of the champagne. The East Egg wife had seemed to be like a diamond, cool and hard by virtue of her wealth, but this was merely a pose, and she showed as much anger as the West Egg wives.

Fitzgerald's impressionistic description of the party has a blend of long shots and close-up scenes. Observed first from Nick's house, we see both the stars and the coloured lights that 'make a Christmas tree of Gatsby's enormous garden' (p. 41). 'The lights grow brighter as the earth lurches away from the sun', and the constantly changing artificial lights create 'a sea-change of faces and voices and colour', as they illuminate the ever-moving crowds and blend them together, creating from a distance the effect of an ever-changing sea. Nick uses the metaphor of 'spectroscopic gaiety' to create the image of a prism, separating light into a whole spectrum of colours.

synaesthesia the fusion of different sense impressions to enhance an experience

Bright primary colours predominate and yellow seems dominant, even the cocktail music is yellow, an example of synaesthesia that suggests bright, cheerful, superficial music with no shadows. The colours are 'gaudy', and Nick stands out because he is dressed in white, possibly symbolising his naivety and his belief in his moral superiority.

This scene is juxtaposed with Nick's observation of 'a wafer of moon...shining over Gatsby's house' (p. 56). Gatsby's dream remains intact and pure, symbolised by the moon rising above the garish lights of his drunken parties that 'blind' people literally and morally.

Pause for **Thought**

Nick describes himself as 'one of the few honest people that I have ever known'. Do you think Fitzgerald intends the reader to think of Nick as 'honest'?

The 'chasms' in the artificial landscape of Manhattan are not gorges made by rivers but the spaces between white skyscrapers. For Nick, New York has a 'racy, adventurous feel...at night' (p. 57); however, like the 'poor young clerks', he is an observer, 'wasting the most poignant moments of night and life'. Through the windows of the many taxis (five deep), he can see people being hurried 'towards gaiety' in the theatre district. This presents an interesting contrast between those living the 'racy' life and the 'haunting loneliness' of the outsiders.

Chapter IV

Nick writes a list of the people he has met at Gatsby's parties. He is driven to Manhattan by Gatsby, who makes outrageous and well-rehearsed claims about his past. Nick is sceptical until Gatsby produces a photograph of himself at Oxford with an earl.

Over lunch, Nick meets Meyer Wolfshiem, the gambler supposedly responsible for fixing the 1919 World Baseball Series. From Wolfshiem Nick learns something of what happened to Gatsby when he returned from the war. Nick sees Tom and goes to introduce the two men, but Gatsby mysteriously disappears.

The scene cuts abruptly to Central Park, where Jordan takes over the narration. She tells Nick how Daisy went out with Gatsby in Louisville, Kentucky, before he went to war in 1917. In June 1919, she married Tom, who was unfaithful to her within three months. We learn that Gatsby bought his house so that he would be across the bay from Daisy, and that he would like to meet her at Nick's bungalow.

Commentary: **Nick is taken to town by Gatsby in his extravagant automobile, 'terraced with a labyrinth of windshields that mirrored a dozen suns' (p. 63) and 'with fenders spread like wings we scattered light through half Astoria' (p. 66). Gatsby has his headlights blazing, even though it is sunny, and his car takes natural light and multiplies it twelvefold, reinforcing the flamboyance of a wealthy man who wants to be noticed.**

From a distance, the city rises 'up across the river in white heaps and sugar lumps' like a fairy-tale landscape with 'its first wild promise of all the mystery and the beauty in the world'. However, even as he marvels at it, Nick is aware that it was 'built with a wish out of nonolfactory money', that those who paid for the buildings had gained their fortunes immorally. As they drive across Queensboro Bridge, 'the sunlight through the girders (made) a constant flicker upon the moving cars' (p. 67), and this contributes to its romantic appearance.

From the bright sunshine of 'roaring noon', the lighting is suddenly changed as we are taken into a cellar in 'half-darkness'. In spite of its prohibition, alcohol is easy to obtain, and business is conducted in illegal drinking dens where people 'coolly' discuss immoral activities. These dens are not only frequented by the underworld; the apparently respectable Tom is also there. The two scenes together create a strong visual image of the two sides of Gatsby: the flamboyant exterior which masks mysterious criminal activities.

Wolfshiem is a professional gambler, a dangerous man who uses a 'heavy' to silence the opposition. This thug is appropriately

Context

Herman Rosenthal
complained to the
press that his illegal
casinos had been badly
damaged because
the police extorted
substantial sums in
exchange for immunity
from police interference.
He was shot in the
street outside the
Metropole. Three years
later, five police officers,
including Lieutenant
Charles Becker, went
to the electric chair for
arranging Rosenthal's
murder. Fitzgerald
makes an extended
reference to this case
on pp. 68–69, providing
real details to set his
characters in context.

Pause for **Thought** ❚❚

Study the colour
illustration of the
front cover of Francis
Cugat's original
dust jacket. Explore
what it tells us about
Nick that he felt he
had to explain that
'I had no girl whose
disembodied face
floated along the dark
cornices and blinding
signs' (p. 78).

named Katspaugh, a homophone for cat's paw. Nick's mocking
anti-Semitism means that Wolfshiem seems quite a comic
character with his 'tragic nose' and his 'business gonnegtion'.
However, Wolfshiem's name brands him a ruthless predator and
his cufflinks suggest sinister associations. Fitzgerald sets him
firmly in the contemporary criminal fraternity by linking him
with 'Rosy' Rosenthal, a real-life gambler who was gunned down
by the police.

After Jordan has finished telling Nick about Daisy's ill-fated love
affair with Gatsby and his plans to revive it, they drive through
Central Park where they hear a popular song about a sheik
with his 'captured bride' and his plans to 'conquer love by fear',
serving as an ironic comment on Gatsby's intentions. In a telling
critique on this age of mass entertainment, Fitzgerald has this
brutal song being inappropriately sung by children.

The Granger Collection/TopFoto

The cover of the first edition of the novel, published in 1925

Chapter V

Gatsby is waiting for Nick on his return. He offers him a little business
on the side, which Nick interprets as an offer 'for services rendered'.
He refuses. Structurally, Nick's tea party is at the centre of the novel. It
rains, but the sun comes out briefly. Gatsby is embarrassed, then filled

with 'unreasoning joy', then 'consumed with wonder at her presence'. He shows Daisy and Nick his house and grounds. Nick wonders whether Daisy can live up to Gatsby's dream of her. He leaves them holding hands in the music room.

Commentary: **Nick returns to West Egg at two o'clock in the morning. Gatsby is waiting to know whether Jordan has persuaded Nick to invite Daisy to visit; he tries to appear nonchalant. His 'house blazed gaudily on' (p. 81) as if to reassure Gatsby that it will impress Daisy, but it looks like 'the World's Fair', somewhere superficially exciting but with no substance to it. As if to reinforce the message that his dream is not pure, the house appears to be winking conspiratorially as he tries to persuade Nick to act as go-between in his seduction of a married woman.**

The day of the tea party, it is raining and the windows are bleared, symbolising Nick's inability to see clearly the immorality of his actions. The rain reflects Gatsby's mood of doubt and apprehension as he sits 'miserably' waiting for Daisy's arrival. Later, however, the sun comes out, reflecting Gatsby's change of mood. The childish synaesthesia in 'twinkle-bells of sunshine' enhances Nick's description of Gatsby as 'an ecstatic patron of recurrent light' (p. 86) and gives a veneer of childlike innocence to the scene.

Daisy is a romantic: she lingers to enjoy the scents of the flowers as they approach Gatsby's house and waxes lyrical at the sunset peeping through the rain. When she sees the shirts, her reaction is to cry 'stormily', a metaphor suggesting there are deep emotions that Nick cannot begin to understand. It is significant that Nick speculates what Gatsby is thinking and tries to interpret his every expression, but reports Daisy's words and actions in a very superficial way. As Fitzgerald once told his publisher, 'it's a man's book'.

Through Daisy's presence, Nick is able to appreciate the romantic atmosphere of the house and garden. When there is no party in full swing, the garden is filled with odours that are 'sparkling', 'frothy', or 'pale gold'. Fitzgerald's use of synaesthesia here fuses the senses of sight and smell to add depth to Nick's appreciation of the flowers. The bedrooms are vivid with new flowers and swathed in rose and lavender silk, subtle, feminine colours that suggest that inside the house is also fragrant and romantic.

> Gatsby's house looks like 'the World's Fair'

Task 2

Write Daisy's account of her visit to Gatsby's house. Try to build upon Fitzgerald's presentation of her character and echo specific aspects of his form, structure and language. Write a brief commentary to accompany your new text which explains how and where you have tried to reflect the original novel. Then you might like to compare your version with the sample response which appears in the *Working with the text* section (p. 85 of this guide).

In Gatsby's bedroom is 'a toilet set of pure dull gold' (p. 89); this association with a precious metal suggests the purity and richness of Gatsby's feelings for her. Daisy is also glowing; the sunlight gleams on her brass buttons and it blinds Gatsby as it is reflected off the brush she is using. Nick describes Gatsby's shirts in subtle pastel shades using colours associated with natural things such as coral, apple-green, lavender and faint orange. Gatsby is wearing a white flannel suit, silver shirt and gold-coloured tie, which could be construed as garish, but also reinforces the idea of his feelings for her being pure, especially as his clothes echo the colours she herself wears so often, which are suggested by her name. Daisy is wearing a lavender hat and her hair, which is naturally blond (pp. 111–12), 'lay like a dash of blue paint across her cheek' (p. 83). Clearly she has dyed her hair, which contradicts Nick's fresh, natural image of her.

It starts to rain again, suggesting, perhaps, that the relationship is doomed. However, 'the darkness had parted in the west, and there was a pink and golden billow of foamy cloud above the sea' (p. 91), a romantic interval in an otherwise threatening sky. Gatsby attempts to banish the gloom by turning on the lights, but in the music room he just turns on 'a solitary lamp'. The flame on the match with which he nervously lights Daisy's cigarette trembles, and he and Daisy sit in the shadows where there is 'no light save what the gleaming floor bounced in from the hall' (p. 92). This is a Romantic image, echoing Keats's 'Ode to a Nightingale', but the light is artificial and thunder can be heard ominously rumbling outside as if Nature herself disapproves. The lighting reinforces the negative note of the songs Klipspringer plays, and reminds us that Gatsby 'had no real right to touch her hand'.

Klipspringer first plays 'The Love Nest' on the piano. This song draws attention to the fact that Gatsby's house is no cosy 'love nest'; the huge, vulgar mansion is more like 'a palace with a gilded dome'. It was not built 'in bygone days' but is a recent factual imitation. Worse than this, Gatsby dismisses his servants and replaces them with Wolfshiem's thugs. Far from being alone, while Daisy and Gatsby conduct their love affair there will be constant reminders of the criminal activities through which Gatsby gained entry to Daisy's world. By evoking the lyrics of this song, Fitzgerald has provided a neatly ironic counterpoint to Gatsby's idealisation of Daisy.

*Pause for **Thought***

Watch the dramatisation of Nick's and Daisy's visit to Gatsby's house from the 1974 film version of the novel. Think about which aspects of the original text you feel this visual interpretation is able to suggest effectively, and in what ways the film fails to capture the essence of the text.

Nick leaves while Klipspringer is playing 'Ain't we got fun', a jolly, popular tune. Fitzgerald quotes from the lyrics to reinforce his message that the careless, hedonistic lifestyle of the rich can only be temporary, 'in between time'. In the next verse — 'Times are bad and getting badder,/ Still we have fun./ There's nothing surer,/ The rich get rich and the poor get — laid off' — the explicit class division offers an ironic commentary on the class difference between Daisy and Gatsby as they are, presumably, about to make love. The lyrics highlight the carelessness of the rich as they joke about the plight of the poor, just as the novel highlights the carelessness of the rich towards the hopelessness of those in the valley of ashes.

> …the novel highlights the carelessness of the rich

Chapter VI

Nick deviates from his plan to tell events in the order in which he learns them and narrates some of what Gatsby tells him the night after Myrtle is killed. We learn that Gatsby was the son of a small farmer. He was dissatisfied with his life, left home and drifted until he met Dan Cody at the age of 17. He apparently spent the next five years living on Cody's yacht, but his account is suspect as he claims the yacht went three times round the continent.

Nick then describes an occasion when Tom and friends rode over to Gatsby's house. Gatsby is a welcoming and generous host, and Mrs Sloane issues an empty invitation which Gatsby gratefully accepts. When he goes to get his car, they rudely ride away.

Tom and Daisy go to Gatsby's next party and Nick senses a 'pervading harshness that hadn't been there before' (p. 100). After the party, Nick interprets in his own words what Gatsby told him of his affair with Daisy in 1917.

Commentary: **Nick's description of Dan Cody helps us to understand the contrast between East and West. Cody made his fortune in the West and 'brought back to the Eastern Seaboard the savage violence of the frontier brothel and saloon' (p. 97). Cody gave Gatsby a taste for wealth and a dubious moral stance on how to obtain it. He epitomises the corrupted American Dream.**

The 'sinister contrast' (p. 10) between East and West Egg could be that the residents of East Egg are unable to seize the day and do live a life of 'euphemisms' in which the truth, like Tom's

Pause for _Thought_ ⏸

Look at a map of North America and consider how likely it is that a luxury yacht would be able to sail 'three times around the continent'.

mistress, is known but not spoken about. A prime example is when Mrs Sloane enthusiastically invites Gatsby and Nick to supper; Nick is familiar with the code and knows she does not mean it, but Gatsby belongs to West Egg and takes her invitation at face value. Nick is outraged at the cruel humiliation inflicted on his friend, putting in an exclamation mark after his bitter comment 'As though they cared!' This incident is an important stage in Nick's relationship with Gatsby.

*Pause for **Thought***

At the first party he describes, Nick mentions five crates of oranges and lemons. This time he notices only the 'fruit rinds and discarded favours and crushed flowers' (p. 106). What does this detail suggest about his feelings?

Nick uses more muted colours for the party than previously. The producer has a 'sort of blue nose'; the 'ghostly' celebrity is 'a gorgeous, scarcely human orchid of a woman', and she sits under 'a white-plum tree'. The morning is 'soft black', and 'sometimes a shadow moved against a dressing-room blind above, gave way to another shadow, an indefinite procession of shadows'. Even the beach is black. Nick thinks that the unpleasantness he feels may be either because he has grown used to the glamour or because he is looking through Daisy's eyes, but it could be because he identifies with Gatsby's humiliation and resents how he is being used by his guests.

Daisy enters into the spirit of the party; she keeps a check on Tom but relaxes once she has established that the girl he is with is no real threat. Once again Nick is complicit in her affair with Gatsby, keeping watch while the lovers retire to his house. Nick speculates that Daisy is offended by the party, assuming that 'she saw something awful in the very simplicity she failed to

Daisy (Mia Farrow) and Tom (Bruce Dern) at one of Gatsby's lavish parties, in the 1974 film

Capital Pictures

understand' (p. 103). However, he offers no evidence of this. West Egg stands for vigour, energy, novelty and escapism, in opposition to the moribund East Egg. Daisy may not approve of the people of West Egg, but she says 'At least they are more interesting than the people we know'.

Nick's perception is that the lives of these newly rich are empty and that a force beyond their control, 'fate', is herding them like cattle 'from nothing to nothing'. However, the implication seems to be that they know this and enjoy their lives with 'raw vigour', without worrying about the future. This seems to be the 'very simplicity' that Daisy failed to understand.

> …'fate' is herding the newly rich 'from nothing to nothing'

As Tom and Daisy go, she looks up at the lighted top of the steps, and Nick thinks she looks reluctant to leave, fearing that Gatsby might fall in love with an 'authentically radiant young girl', showing that Nick thinks Daisy's own radiance is a pose. However, it may be that she just envies the women at the party for their independence.

When Gatsby's parties have fulfilled their purpose and attracted Daisy, he will not have any more, so 'Three o'clock in the Morning', a 'neat, sad little waltz', just before dawn, seems appropriate. When Daisy leaves the party with Tom, in spite of the 'romantic possibilities' offered by the song and by Gatsby, Fitzgerald foreshadows the end of their love story. The sad mood of the song reflects Gatsby's 'unutterable depression' as he tells Nick: 'I feel far away from her…It's hard to make her understand.' He thinks they can re-create the past, but he ignores the fact that she is a wife and mother, so there can be no 'honeymoon', as there will be for the couple in the song.

Context

Fitzgerald wrote: 'That's the whole burden of the novel — the loss of those illusions that give such color to the world that you don't care whether things are true or false as long as they partake of the magical glory' (letter of 1924, after his wife, Zelda, had had an affair).

Chapter VII

On the hottest day of the summer, Nick has lunch at the Buchanans'. Daisy seems to be trying to provoke a crisis by her behaviour and Tom guesses the truth. Aimlessly, they drive to Manhattan, with Daisy and Gatsby in Tom's car and Jordan, Nick and Tom in Gatsby's car. Tom stops at Wilson's garage for petrol and Myrtle sees him.

In the unbearable heat in the Plaza Hotel, tensions rise and Tom challenges Gatsby to explain himself. Gatsby tries to make Daisy say that she never loved Tom, but she cannot do this. Nevertheless, she does say she is leaving Tom and this provokes him to give details of

Gatsby's criminal activities. Gatsby ends up 'defending his name against accusations that had not been made' (p. 128). This frightens Daisy and she draws into herself, now unable to do anything. Tom, realising he has won, scornfully tells Daisy to go home with Gatsby, and they leave.

Nick's narrative uses the evidence of Michaelis at the inquest to fill in the details of what happened before Myrtle recognised the car that Tom had been driving earlier and rushed out to her death. Michaelis gave a graphic description of the body. Nick then resumes his supposed eye-witness account of their arrival at the garage, where Myrtle is already dead. A witness tells the police that she was hit by a big yellow car.

Back at the Buchanans', Nick resists invitations to go in. He sees Gatsby watching the house. From what Gatsby says, he guesses that Daisy was driving. He peeps into the house, sees Daisy and Tom together and concludes that Gatsby is watching over nothing.

Commentary: **Nick's reference to Gatsby as Trimalchio links *The Great Gatsby* with Eliot's *The Waste Land*, which has a quotation from the 'Satyricon' as the epigraph. In Eliot's chosen extract, the vulgar, nouveau-riche narrator describes how he saw the Cumaean Sybil in a glass bottle being taunted by boys who asked what she wanted. When Apollo had granted her a wish, she had asked for as many years of life as she held grains of sand in her hand. However, she forgot to ask for continuous youth. Both writers foresee the dangers in a barren life that is concerned only with material things and has no spiritual dimension.**

Nick assumes that Myrtle thinks Jordan is Tom's wife when she looks at the car 'with jealous terror', however, she has probably seen pictures of Daisy in society magazines, so it is more likely that she fears that Tom has a new mistress. Fitzgerald describes her in detail after the accident and insisted to his publisher that he did not want to change the wording. (For a close analysis of this description see *Working with the text*.)

Fitzgerald makes his readers feel the heat. He takes us inside the Buchanans' house where 'the room, shadowed well with awnings, was dark and cool'; the dining-room too was 'darkened against the heat'. However, Fitzgerald needs the heat to shorten tempers, so the party travels to Manhattan, where there is no cool refuge. The heat is oppressive, exacerbating the tension in the atmosphere. As the men wait for the women, Nick notices 'a silver curve of the moon' already in the western sky, but the brightness of the sun will symbolically drain this romantic image of any light at all. As they stop for petrol, the 'broad glare'

Context

Fitzgerald thought of calling the novel 'Trimalchio at West Egg'. Trimalchio is the narrator of the 'Satyricon' by Petronius, a satire on Roman life in the first century AD. He was a freed slave who became wealthy and was renowned for his excessively lavish parties.

of afternoon sunlight makes Wilson, who has found out about Myrtle's affair, look appropriately green.

When the row that has been brewing at the Plaza eventually erupts, Gatsby appears 'content', but Daisy looks 'desperately from one to the other', although earlier she seemed to be trying to provoke it. Perhaps the music has reminded her why she married Tom and rekindled the love she had for him then. Put on the spot, she realises that she and Tom share happy, tender memories that she cannot deny. When Tom starts giving details of how Gatsby made his money, Daisy is 'terrified'. Confronted with his illegal and amoral activities, she draws back into herself. When Gatsby reveals even more crimes by defending himself 'against accusations that had not been made', she turns to Tom to protect her. It seems she had wanted love and romance, not a life of sordid crime. She is 'alarmed' when Tom insists she drive back with Gatsby. She is vulnerable, but Tom is using her as a trophy, showing off his victory by insisting that she spend time alone with his rival.

Confused and alarmed, Daisy asks to drive, possibly to steady her nerves, as Gatsby claims. Gatsby's car is large and powerful and this is the first time Daisy has driven it, so it is not surprising that she finds it difficult to control in a crisis. When Myrtle runs out, Daisy hesitates — first swerving away from the woman into the path of the oncoming car and then back to avoid a collision. When she hits Myrtle she steps on the accelerator and cannot stop the car, either out of fear or because she cannot control the vehicle. When Gatsby pulls on the emergency brake, she collapses, clearly emotionally overwrought.

When Tom, Nick and Jordan reach the scene, it is evening. The garage is 'lit only by a yellow light in a swinging metal basket overhead'. As the light swings, Nick sees Wilson swaying in the doorway of his office. Wilson seems mesmerised by the light, looking from it to Myrtle and then back, calling out incessantly: 'Oh, my Ga-od!' This foreshadows the fragment that Michaelis describes, when the eyes of Dr Eckleburg begin to emerge in the dawn light, and Wilson repeats 'God sees everything' (p. 152). The lighting of both scenes suggests that Wilson feels a need for something to give meaning to life and death, but there is no God, only an artificial light and an advertisement.

At the Buchanans' mansion, 'two windows bloomed with light'. The use of the word 'bloom' suggests a natural flower-like

*Pause for **Thought***

Fitzgerald criticised his portrayal of Daisy in Chapter VII, saying: 'I've worried about it too long and I can't quite place Daisy's reaction.' Do you think he was right to worry about his portrayal of Daisy?

quality, but it is electric light, in contrast with the moonlight outside. The lighting associates Daisy with the illusion of romance, whereas Gatsby is bathed in moonlight so that his pink suit is luminous, as he watches over her in a sacred 'vigil'.

Jordan swallows her pride and twice invites Nick in. He has led her to believe that his intentions are serious, even taking the trouble to 'ingratiate' himself with her aunt (p. 98), and now, when she needs him, he fails her. Nick, however, blames her.

Pause for **Thought**

How far do you agree with Nick that Gatsby is 'watching over nothing'?

Through the pantry window, 'a small rectangle of light', Nick sees Daisy and Tom and assumes that for Daisy the romance is over and she has returned to her safe, rich world, leaving Gatsby, symbolically lit by moonlight, 'watching over nothing'. Fitzgerald's use of the moon associates Gatsby with romantic heroes and pure love, while the artificial light that draws Tom and Daisy together suggests that Daisy has betrayed her lover.

Chapter VIII

Before dawn, Nick walks across to Gatsby's house. Nick paraphrases what Gatsby tells him about his wartime love affair with Daisy and what he did when he returned from the war. Nick feels close to Gatsby as he leaves, saying: 'They're a rotten crowd...You're worth the whole damn bunch put together.' At the office, Jordan phones asking to see him. He declines. He tries unsuccessfully to phone Gatsby four times.

Once again Nick deviates from his plan and tells us what he learned later, at the inquest and from the newspapers. He gives the details of Wilson's movements on the day after Myrtle was killed, however, he withholds the information that Wilson called at the Buchanans' house.

Nick then reconstructs Gatsby's last movements and tries to imagine what he was feeling as he lay on the air-bed. Although Nick was one of the people who found Gatsby, he gives no description of the body, and mentions only that the gardener found Wilson's body, so we are given no graphic descriptions of these violent deaths.

Top ten **quotation** ❯

Commentary: **The darkest hour is just before dawn, when the moon has set, as Gatsby clutches 'at some last hope'. With only the glow of the cigarettes illuminating their faces, Gatsby tells Nick the story of how he came to be following a 'grail' (p. 142), like the heroes of medieval romances. At dawn, Fitzgerald is very specific about the quality of the 'grey-turning, gold-turning' light that fills the house, a gloomy light, but still with a hint of gold to suggest the possibility of romance.**

The song that tempted Daisy back on to the dance floor after the war was 'Beale Street Blues', a lament that Prohibition threatened the very life of the centre of vibrant African-American culture in Memphis, Tennessee. In Beale Street, music expressed the dreams and the heartache of people who had recently been slaves. This was where the Blues were born, before becoming popular with young white Americans. This reference reminds the reader of the exclusiveness of the American Dream, only available for those of north European origin.

In a description of Gatsby's smile, Nick juxtaposes the rapturous word 'ecstatic', derived from the ancient Greek word for standing outside oneself, with the rough slang term 'cahoots' (p. 147). This phrase neatly sums up Nick's perception of Gatsby, the 'elegant young rough-neck' with the sublime dream. However, the fact that Nick does not think they have been in league with each other all along reveals that he neither realises how he has been used nor admits his part in the affair.

After Gatsby's death, Nick assumes that he was waiting for a phone call from Daisy, and speculates that 'Gatsby himself didn't believe it would come, and perhaps he no longer cared'. However, Fitzgerald creates mystery because, when Nick tried to phone Gatsby that morning, 'the wire was being kept open for a long distance from Detroit'. Perhaps Daisy did try to phone. Perhaps Gatsby was still waiting for the call from Detroit.

When Jordan telephones Nick the following day, her voice, usually fresh and cool, 'seemed harsh and dry' over the phone. This suggests that she is in a highly charged emotional state, either because of whatever happened in the Buchanan house the previous night, or because she still has not recovered from the shock of Myrtle's death, or because Nick failed to support her, or a combination of all three. She gives him an opportunity to make amends by saying: 'You weren't so nice to me last night.' After his insensitive reply: 'How could it have mattered then?' she is silent, perhaps wondering how to express her need for him without appearing vulnerable. She phrases her request in the most denotative way: 'However — I want to see you', so that he does not know how hurt she is.

Fitzgerald employs dramatic irony when Nick replies, 'I want to see you, too' because we know he is lying. She takes his words at face value and suggests abandoning her plans to go to Southampton, revealing how desperately she needs to see him.

> ...the exclusiveness of the American Dream

Pause for _Thought_

Do you think it was Nick or Jordan who hung up the receiver? What makes you think this?

Context

Southampton is a town on Long Island, and is the home of the National Golf Links of America.

Task 4

Write one of the contemporary newspaper accounts of Gatsby's death. Try to echo specific aspects of Fitzgerald's form, structure and language as far as possible. You might wish to write a brief commentary to accompany your new text which explains how and where you have tried to reflect the original novel.

He declines; she accepts his decision. Nick is annoyed by the fact that Jordan has left Daisy's house, but he does not ask her why. In fact, Jordan went because Daisy and Tom left the house after Tom told Wilson where to find the driver of the yellow car.

Chapter IX

Nick apparently spent a year constructing his account of events. In the rest of the novel he tells what he remembers. He refers to the inquest and to learning that Daisy and Tom had gone away. He gives details of his attempts to persuade Wolfshiem to go to the funeral and describes a strange phone call that implicated Gatsby in a bond fraud. On the third day, Gatsby's father arrived and details of Gatsby's early life are revealed.

Nick decides to go back to the Midwest. He says goodbye to Jordan and he challenges Tom about sending Wilson to Gatsby but then shakes his hand. He visits Gatsby's deserted house. Lying on the shore in the moonlight, he has a vision of Long Island as it would have looked to the Dutch sailors who first discovered it, 'a fresh green breast' promising a new life, just as the green light at the end of Daisy's dock had promised Gatsby that he could achieve his dream. Nick realises that, although these dreams are for ever out of reach because they are based on a vision of lost innocence, it will not stop us striving for them.

Commentary: **Wolfshiem claims that he and Gatsby were closely involved in everything, 'always together'. However, it is significant that he refuses to go to Gatsby's funeral, not wanting to 'get mixed up in it in any way'.**

Gatsby's father is 'a solemn old man' who is clearly proud of his son. It may have been he who made James Gatz ambitious as he is convinced that, had his son lived, he would have 'helped build up the country'. His dream, like that of the Founding Fathers, was to make America great.

Context

The Founding Fathers were the American leaders who signed the Declaration of Independence (1776) and who drew up the United States Constitution 11 years later.

As Nick thinks of returning to the Midwest, where old traditions and family values have offered him security in the past, he recalls other times when he returned home from school and college. He remembers a sense of collective belonging, which is revealed in his use of plural first person possessive determiners — 'our identity with this country', 'our snow' — and a personal attachment with 'my Middle West', 'I am part of that'. His memories are of friends, Christmas festivities and long train journeys. However, what he remembers is not so much the reality but a Christmas card scene that suggests the

innocent world of childhood when even long train journeys were 'thrilling'.

He remembers that, when he returned from the war, the East had excited him, making him 'keenly aware of its superiority to the bored, sprawling, swollen towns beyond the Ohio'. At that time, he found the Midwest stifling with the 'interminable inquisitions', as the members of his extended family asked his intentions and when he was going to marry the girl to whom he had written weekly letters signed 'Love, Nick' (p. 59). At that time, the East had offered a fresh start, but 'after Gatsby's death the East was haunted' (p. 167) for him like the nightmare scenes El Greco painted, so he decided to 'come back home', the verb 'come' rather than 'go' suggesting that once again he feels that the Midwest is where he belongs. Using the pathetic fallacy, Fitzgerald projects Nick's mood onto the 'sullen' sky, and the moon is 'lustreless', with no suggestion of romance.

When Nick seeks Jordan out to end the relationship, he nervously talks 'over and around what had happened', while she lies perfectly still listening. Once again, her chin is 'raised a little jauntily', and the reader recognises the familiar sign that she is adopting a mask. She has planned her defensive strategy and tells him that she is engaged to another man. However, when he gets up to leave, she suddenly blurts out how much he hurt her by throwing her over. She says 'I don't give a damn about you now' (p. 168) — an admission that she did care for him then. She accuses him of not being honest and straightforward, as he pretends, but refuses to allow herself to be dragged into an argument. She has let her guard down a little, enough to make him 'angry', but retained her dignity. Nick feels threatened by her poise, her detachment, her independence.

The final fragment that Fitzgerald offers us is of Nick's last night in West Egg, looking out over the Sound. As the moon rises higher and shines more brightly, the details of the scene fade away until he has a vision of what the island must have looked like when the Dutch sailors first arrived. He imagines how they felt when they saw 'a fresh, green breast of the new world. Its vanished trees…had once pandered in whispers to the last and greatest of all human dreams'. Here Fitzgerald fuses the dreams of the first explorers with Gatsby's dream 'when he first picked out the green light at the end of Daisy's dock', and then the light becomes a symbol of the American Dream of 'the orgastic future that year by year recedes before us'.

Taking it ▶
Further ▶

El Greco (The Greek) was a Renaissance painter, sculptor and architect who lived in Spain for much of his life. He is best known for tortuously elongated figures, his dramatic use of colour and his perturbed, violent and apparently careless style of painting. See his *View of Toledo* on: www.ibiblio.org/wm/paint/auth/greco/toledo.jpg.

pathetic fallacy
attributing emotions to inanimate objects, usually elements of nature, to represent the persona's feelings

❮ Top ten *quotation*

❮ Top ten *quotation*

Themes

As this diagram shows, the themes are all interlinked and crucial to them all is the fact that the novel is set at a particular time in history, shortly after the First World War.

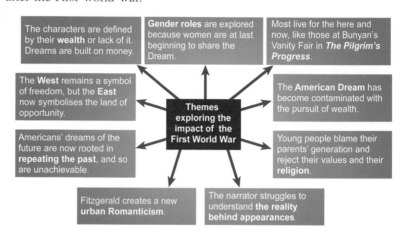

The characters are defined by their **wealth** or lack of it. Dreams are built on money.

Gender roles are explored because women are at last beginning to share the Dream.

Most live for the here and now, like those at Bunyan's Vanity Fair in *The Pilgrim's Progress*.

The **West** remains a symbol of freedom, but the **East** now symbolises the land of opportunity.

Themes exploring the impact of the First World War

The **American Dream** has become contaminated with the pursuit of wealth.

Americans' dreams of the future are now rooted in **repeating the past**, and so are unachievable.

Young people blame their parents' generation and reject their values and their **religion**.

Fitzgerald creates a new **urban Romanticism**.

The narrator struggles to understand **the reality behind appearances**.

The American Dream

Context

Daniel Boone was famous for winning what is now known as the state of Kentucky from the Native Americans. Buffalo Bill Cody was a soldier and showman, among other things. He earned his nickname by killing 4,280 buffalo in 18 months.

The American Dream is rooted in the American Declaration of Independence (see Historical context, p. 61 of this guide) and its insistence on 'all men' having the right to the 'Pursuit of Happiness' and in the desire of immigrants to create a land of opportunity. The pioneer in *The Great Gatsby*, Dan Cody, 'a token of forgotten violence' (p. 157), bears the names of two of the legendary heroes of frontier life, Daniel Boone and Bill Cody.

Fitzgerald makes no attempt to romanticise his portrait of Cody, who would seem to be the antithesis of the American Dream, yet in fact he represents the hard reality. If happiness is defined as a 'right' and regarded as an entitlement like 'life' and 'liberty', then the Declaration of Independence can be interpreted as justifying the actions of those who pursue wealth at any cost. Cody's wealth was supposedly 'a product of the Nevada silver fields, of the Yukon, of every rush for metal since seventy-five' (p. 96). Prospecting did create millionaires, but the mania to get rich brought out the worst in human nature. In the twentieth century, men like Jay Gatsby got rich quickly, but Fitzgerald shows that his methods sit uneasily with the romance of his dream.

Wealth

The Great Gatsby is full of money and the reader is permitted to glimpse the extravagant lifestyle of the fabulously wealthy. However, Fitzgerald has exposed the reality behind the façade. In this society everyone is defined by their wealth and when it was acquired. There is a sharp division between the inhabitants of East Egg with their 'old money' and those of West Egg with 'new money', but both are going from 'nothing to nothing'. Both communities live in close proximity to the desperate poverty of those in the valley of ashes and have to travel through the valley every time they go into New York.

New York was built with 'nonolfactory money', which has a bad smell because it has been acquired illegally. Nick's family's money comes from a business built up when his great-uncle paid for a substitute to fight for him in the American Civil War. Tom is from Chicago, so it is most likely that his family made their money in the infamous meat trade. Gatsby's dream is built on the money he has to acquire to reach Daisy, but his methods of acquiring it frighten her away.

Manhattan is the financial centre and that is where Nick is learning about the bond business. Although the word suggests honour and dependability, bonds are only a substitute for real money, and in the 1920s they were sold 'on the margin', to people who could not afford to pay for them but intended to pay their creditor out of the profits when the shares were sold. New York is also where the gambler and criminal businessman, Meyer Wolfshiem, has his office.

Three O'Clock in the Morning

The Sensational Dance Hit of Two Continents

Words by Dorothy Terriss
Music by Julian Robledo

*Copyright By West's Ltd, London, England
Published In America By Leo Feist Inc, New York*

Dance music flourished in the nightclubs frequented by the wealthy. The song 'Three o'clock in the morning' is mentioned in Chapter VI.

Context

During the American Civil War (1861–65), 11 Southern slave-owning states seceded from the United States and formed the Confederacy, which fought against the United States (the Union). The South was heavily defeated and slavery was officially abolished throughout America.

East and West

Early settlers from Europe travelled west to the New World. For Americans, the West has always been a powerful symbol of opportunity and freedom. Going west was always seen as following the path of the sun and therefore the setting in the west is the end of the trail and the pioneers' journeys, their hopes and dreams. However, life for the pioneers who pushed forward the frontier of civilisation in the Wild West was hard and the law was difficult to enforce, so they developed a distinctive American spirit, very different from those who remained in the East, where the influence of the Old World was stronger.

The pioneers were survivors and Nick suggests that the harshness of their lives had destroyed their sense of the 'fundamental decencies'. When the continent was 'tamed', its mineral wealth exploited and the West Coast populated, there were no longer so many opportunities to make one's fortune, so the same ruthless men turned east. The financial and business world on the Eastern Seaboard came to symbolise the opportunity to make lots of money quickly.

Repeating the past

The Romantic poets were fascinated by time and Keats especially explored different ways of trying to defeat time in his poetry. Fitzgerald takes up this theme of the Romantics and explores humanity's attempts to repeat the past. Jay Gatsby has rewritten his past, manipulated time once when he reinvented himself (p. 95), and he dreams of doing it again.

Nick also wants to go back to the clear-cut moral world of wartime (p. 8). He dreams of returning home on the train (pp. 166–67), as he had done as a youth, and finding again the old familiar traditions and moral values he had grown up with.

Nick 'felt that Tom would drift on forever seeking, a little wistfully, for the dramatic turbulence of some irrecoverable football game' (p. 12).

The man who built Gatsby's house tried to bribe his neighbours to participate in his recreation of the past. They refused (p. 85). He has faithfully recreated 'a factual imitation of some Hôtel de Ville in Normandy' (p. 11), but it is a 'huge incoherent failure of a house' (p. 171), a description that underlines the futility of Gatsby's dream of repeating the past.

Taking it
Further

An Hôtel de Ville is a city or town hall. To see an image of a typical Normandy Hôtel de Ville check out:
http://static.panoramio.com/photos/original/5545325.jpg

Urban Romanticism

Fitzgerald chose to have a narrator with a romantic imagination so that, when Nick sees Gatsby's photograph, he enthuses, 'it was all true. I saw the skins of tigers flaming in his palace on the Grand Canal; I saw him opening a chest of rubies to ease, with their crimson-lighted depths, the gnawings of his broken heart' (pp. 65–66). This choice allows Fitzgerald to gloss over the means by which Gatsby became rich and concentrate on his dream.

Nick, however, is not a Romantic in the nineteenth-century tradition; Fitzgerald reconstructed Romanticism to fit 1920s urban America. Nick describes New York with its 'white chasms', created by tall buildings, in 'the enchanted metropolitan twilight' (p. 57), and he finds Romantic images indoors, such as his description of how the wind blew the curtains 'like pale flags, twisting them up toward the frosted wedding-cake of the ceiling, and then rippled over the wine-coloured rug, making a shadow on it as wind does on the sea' (p. 13).

When Daisy imagines that she sees a nightingale, she knows that it is not native to America and must have 'come over on the Cunard or White Star Line' (p. 20), a symbolic acknowledgement that Romanticism has had to adapt to American culture. Nevertheless, it gives insight into the sadness beneath her 'tense gaiety', and the suggestion of her longing for romantic love adds pathos to the scene where the 'fifth guest's shrill metallic urgency' (p. 21) will not let her forget that her husband has a mistress.

Fitzgerald echoes 'Ode to a Nightingale' when Daisy and Nick visit Gatsby's house. While Keats listens to the bird's song, he is lying under trees. The moon is out 'But here there is no light,/Save what from heaven is with the breezes blown'. Nick observes that Daisy and Gatsby sit in a dark corner of the room 'where there was no light save what the gleaming floor bounced in from the hall' (p. 92). Instead of moonlight coming down from 'heaven', the light from an electric bulb in the hall is reflected upwards. Instead of the light being 'blown' naturally on the breezes, it is 'bounced' like a solid man-made object. As well as creating an urban Romantic moment, the echo helps Fitzgerald evoke the significance of the moment for the two lovers as they are alone for the first time for five years.

Context

In classical mythology, Philomel, a tragic victim of male lust and brutality, was turned into a nightingale, so, as well as being a romantic image, the bird carries associations with tragedy. So do the Cunard and White Star Lines, because of the sinking of the *Lusitania* and the *Titanic*.

Task 5

Find other examples of Fitzgerald's use of contemporary technology to evoke romantic images. Explore what you think he has achieved by doing so.

Appearance and reality

Nick's view

Nick reports his sense impressions as events unfold, but he struggles to understand the reality behind them. He is our eyes; we see only what he notices and comments on. Nick is, by nature, an onlooker. At the Buchanans' house, he wants to give the impression of being frank and open, 'to look squarely at every one, and yet to avoid all eyes' (pp. 20–21), not wanting to get involved. Incomprehensibly, he tells us that his instinct was to telephone for the police. A hint of an explanation may be found in the following paragraph. Tom and Jordan stroll back into the library, 'as if to a vigil beside a perfectly tangible body'. To the over-imaginative Nick, the telephone call has killed something, and Tom and Jordan are going to keep watch and say prayers over it. Fitzgerald seems to be signalling to his readers that Nick has a tendency for hyperbole, and we should not take everything he says too literally.

In New York, he watches with a 'restless eye' and imagines assignations with romantic women (p. 57). When Tom and Daisy come to one of Gatsby's parties, he feels an unpleasantness in the air and speculates that he is looking at the party, and at West Egg itself, through Daisy's eyes: 'It is invariably saddening to look through new eyes at things upon which you have expended your own powers of adjustment' (pp. 100–01). These remind the reader that he is not an omniscient narrator and that everything he writes is filtered through his own vision and insight, or lack of it.

After Gatsby's death, Nick realises that 'the East was haunted for me… distorted beyond my eyes' power of correction' (p. 167), reminding the reader once again that we are reading Nick's interpretation, filtered through his defective vision. Finally, sprawled out on the beach, he broods 'on the old, unknown world', trying to see through the eyes of the pioneering Dutch sailors.

Windows

Fitzgerald continues to investigate the gap between appearance and reality by making numerous references to windows. In each one the observer's vision may have been distorted, and Fitzgerald seems to be warning his readers to mistrust the perceptions of his narrator, who thinks 'life is much more successfully looked at from a single window' (p. 10). This increases the mystery and ambiguity surrounding events.

…Nick's interpretation, filtered through his defective vision

Top ten *quotation* ❯

The 'labyrinth of wind-shields' in Gatsby's car (p. 63) acts like a maze of mirrors reflecting a dozen suns. It is as if they are in 'a conservatory', with no awareness of what is happening outside on the road. Later, looking through the window of Gatsby's house, Daisy thinks the clouds look solid enough to support Gatsby's weight (p. 91). Daisy romantically imagines she can keep Gatsby as a sort of doll, to play with when she wants to. Myrtle looks out of a window at the garage and sees Tom with another woman (p. 119). However, what appears to be the truth that the other woman is his wife or a new mistress is actually an illusion.

After the accident, Nick peers through the pantry window at Tom and Daisy (p. 138). He thinks he sees 'intimacy' between Tom and Daisy, but 'anyone' might disagree that they are 'conspiring together'; they are not holding hands, Tom's hand covers Daisy's, so it is more likely he is taking charge. Again, Wilson looks through the window at the faded advertisement for Dr T. J. Eckleburg and believes that the eyes belong to God, but these eyes are blind (p. 152). Wilson is taken in by the appearance, but the reader understands the reality. While the people who live in the valley of ashes are losing their dreams and dying, turning into ash or dust, Eckleburg will ironically live on and survive to represent the age of materialism.

Religion

Fitzgerald had a strongly religious, Catholic upbringing, and, although he chose to leave the church at the age of 21, there is a powerful spiritual element at work in this novel. He exposes the emptiness beneath the glittering sophistication of postwar America and he invokes religion to demonstrate it.

> ...the emptiness beneath the glittering sophistication

The most explicitly religious reference comes when Wilson looks at the eyes of Dr T. J. Eckleburg and tells Michaelis how he told Myrtle: 'God knows what you've been doing, everything you've been doing. You may fool me, but you can't fool God!' (p. 152). The fact that Wilson equates an advertisement with God suggests that spiritual values have been replaced by empty, meaningless images.

There are several references directly linking Gatsby with Christianity. He claims that what he tells Nick about his past is 'God's truth' and 'his right hand suddenly ordered divine retribution to stand by' (p. 63). However, everything he tells Nick is either an obvious lie or it is disproved later in the novel. Nick claims 'He was a son of God — a phrase which, if it means anything, means just that — and he must be about His Father's business, the service of a vast, vulgar and meretricious beauty' (p. 95).

Fitzgerald's use of capitalisation and the fact that the phrases are taken verbatim from the Bible clearly signal that he wants to link Gatsby with Christ. This reference, however, must be ironic. His adopted father is Cody, an unscrupulous self-made millionaire, so 'His Father's business' must be amassing a fortune by any means.

Nick says that Gatsby 'knew that when he kissed this girl, and forever wed his unutterable visions to her perishable breath, his mind would never romp again like the mind of God' (p. 107); suggesting that this was the moment when Gatsby abandoned his lofty ambitions in order to pursue wealth so that he could win Daisy. If that is what Nick means, then Fitzgerald has shown us that he is mistaken, as Gatsby dedicated himself to the pursuit of worldly wealth before he met Daisy, when he changed his name and rowed out to Cody's yacht.

It must be significant that Gatsby shoulders his own mattress as he walks to his death, dies at about three o'clock in the afternoon, the same hour as Christ was crucified, and 'on the third day' his father comes and his true identity is revealed (p. 158).

However, these religious references say more about the narrator, Nick Carraway, than they do about the eponymous hero. Although Nick clearly had a very religious upbringing and has a strong moral code, it seems that he no longer believes in God. He appears to be searching for something to fill that spiritual need in his life when he meets Gatsby. What attracts him to Gatsby is his 'extraordinary gift for hope, a romantic readiness' (p. 8). Like Christ, Gatsby offers the promise of something better, 'the orgastic future that year by year recedes before us'.

Top ten *quotation* ❯

The seven deadly sins

Further evidence of Nick's religious background can be found in his illustrations of the seven deadly sins. For instance:

Pride

Tom says: 'It's up to us, who are the dominant race, to watch out or these other races will have control of things' (p. 18). Fitzgerald exposes the lie that the American Dream is open to all, because those who have power work to keep it.

Task 6

Find evidence of some of the other sins: gluttony, lust, avarice, wrath and sloth.

Envy

Gatsby 'took Daisy one still October night, took her because he had no real right to touch her hand' (p. 142). Fitzgerald exposes a materialistic society based on envy, in which everyone covets something they have not got, everyone wants to get rich, or, if they are rich, preserve their position against the newly rich.

The seven cardinal virtues

Nick observes that 'everyone suspects himself of at least one of the cardinal virtues' (p. 59) and claims that his virtue is honesty.

Faith

Nick says of Wolfshiem that 'It never occurred to me that one man could start to play with the faith of fifty million people' (p. 71). Fitzgerald's use of the word 'faith' here is ironic, as God has been replaced by sport and the desire to make money by betting on its outcome.

Nick says of Gatsby that 'I had one of those renewals of complete faith in him that I'd experienced before' (p. 123). Nick's faith is not in God but in Gatsby.

Hope

Nick writes that Gatsby had 'an extraordinary gift for hope, a romantic readiness such as I have never found in any other person and which it is not likely I shall ever find again' (p. 8). However, Gatsby's hope is not in a spiritual heaven, but that another man's wife will declare her love for him.

Nick expresses an awareness of something better, but seems to have no hope of his own, except to learn 'the shining secrets that only Midas and Morgan and Maecenas knew' (p. 10), how to make money.

'The World's Fair' (p. 79)

Since 1678 when John Bunyan wrote *The Pilgrim's Progress*, the concept of society being a 'fair' has frequently been employed by writers. Thackeray clearly explains this metaphor in *Vanity Fair* (1847): 'Vanity Fair is a very vain, wicked, foolish place, full of all sorts of humbugs and falsenesses and pretensions.'

Fitzgerald first intended his short story 'Absolution' to be the prologue to *The Great Gatsby*, giving insights into his eponymous hero's upbringing. In this story, a priest tells a boy to go and observe a 'glittering' amusement park, but not to get up close 'because if you do you'll only feel the heat and the sweat and the life.' However, the boy, 'sat there, half terrified...but underneath his terror he felt that...there was something ineffably gorgeous somewhere that had nothing to do with God.'

Task 7

Explore the novel for evidence of the other virtues: prudence, love, justice, fortitude, temperance.

Context

In Bunyan's novel, Vanity Fair was a fair selling vanities, in the town of Vanity . It offers his hero, Christian, worldly pleasures to tempt him away from his pilgrimage to the Celestial City.

Fitzgerald uses words and images from the semantic field of circus and carnival to show that Nick is attracted to the 'ineffably gorgeous' World's Fair, but is aware of its falseness and later feels only 'the heat and the sweat'. Here are some other examples that Fitzgerald has used.

- The epigraph to the book (p. 5), taken from Fitzgerald's *This Side of Paradise*, suggests that Gatsby has to act like a circus performer and become the 'gold-hatted, high-bouncing lover' in order to win Daisy.
- At Gatsby's parties, there are 'enough coloured lights to make a Christmas tree of Gatsby's enormous garden', and the salads have 'harlequin designs' (p. 41).
- Gatsby's guests 'conducted themselves according to the rules of behaviour associated with an amusement park' (p. 43).
- Nick tells us that Gatsby's 'career as Trimalchio was over' (p. 108). Trimalchio threw lavish parties and sought to impress his guests with all manner of excesses. (See Context box on p. 20 of this guide.)
- Nick notes that 'the whole caravansary had fallen in like a card house at the disapproval in her [Daisy's] eyes' (p. 109).
- From this point on, Nick no longer uses the language of the fairground; he seems obsessed with 'the heat and the sweat', although Tom refers to Gatsby's car as 'this circus wagon' (p. 115). Nick has realised at last that what appears 'ineffably gorgeous' has 'nothing to do with God' ('Absolution').

Context

The epigraph is attributed to Thomas Parke D'Invilliers. However, he was a fictional character in Fitzgerald's *This Side of Paradise*.

Nick seems obsessed with 'the heat and the sweat'

Gender roles

Female roles

During the First World War, women had become used to filling the men's roles in the workplace; they had more freedom and financial independence. The rapid growth in mass-produced cars gave them the opportunity for greater mobility, and new technology created celebrities in entertainment and sport. The original wording of the Declaration of Independence promised the Dream to men, but, in the Roaring Twenties, it became possible for women to pursue it.

Jordan Baker

Fitzgerald named Jordan Baker after two automobile manufacturers, so her name fits well with a girl who has taken full advantage of the opportunities for women in postwar America and become a professional sportswoman. There is tension, however, because the male characters have traditional attitudes and disapprove of her emancipation.

Context

Edward S. Jordan manufactured smart luxury cars aimed at women. The Baker Company manufactured electric automobiles, which held many land speed and distance records in the early 1900s.

Daisy Buchanan

As an unmarried woman, Daisy had her own car and was able to work voluntarily for the Red Cross, which meant that she was not under constant supervision. However, Daisy grew up in the old-fashioned world of Kentucky, and she belongs to a class in which women were still not expected to support themselves. Marriage was the only appropriate way for her to break away from parental control. As a married woman, Daisy has less freedom as she has no car of her own.

Myrtle Wilson

Myrtle is poor and the only way she can change her situation is through a man. For ten years she has tried to persuade her husband to go west, so when she meets the handsome and obviously rich Tom Buchanan, and he propositions her, she sees an opportunity to lift herself out of the despairing environment that is the valley of ashes.

Male roles

Fitzgerald also explores a range of men's roles. Tom represents a powerful patriarchy strongly resisting social change. Nick's sexuality is not made clear. Daisy describes him as a 'rose'; Myrtle points him out as someone to whom it is incredible that she could ever be attracted. Nick is attracted to Jordan because she is 'like a young cadet', and he has a strange encounter with Chester McKee, 'a pale, feminine man'.

*Pause for **Thought***

What are the most important themes of the film version you have watched? How do these compare with those of the novel?

Characters

Jay Gatsby

The eponymous hero was born James Gatz, the son of struggling farm people in the Midwest, but in his imagination he always believed they were not his real parents. He left home at 16 and changed his name at 17 when he teamed up with Dan Cody. He met Daisy at training camp, when his poor background was disguised by an officer's uniform, and they had a brief but passionate affair. He fought in the Great War and, on his return, went to New York to become rich so that he would be in the same circle as Daisy, because he hoped to recreate the past. In the novel's present, he is a mysterious character, fabulously wealthy, who throws lavish parties in the hopes of meeting Daisy again. He is presented as a romantic idealist who engages in criminal activities to fund the pursuit of his dream. Gatsby's smile gives the impression of a man of rare charm who makes people feel special, but, when he stops smiling, Nick perceives an uncultured but ultra-polite young man who speaks with studied formality in order to conceal his origins. At several points in the novel, Gatsby's mask slips, giving Nick a glimpse of the hard man at the heart of the romantic dreamer e.g. 'he looked as if he had "killed a man"' (p. 128).

Gatsby's speech is revealed as a pose because he repeatedly calls all the men he meets by the unfashionable epithet 'old sport'. He uses no figurative language and no complex syntax, often lapsing into incomplete utterances. He uses a lot of clichés such as 'lived like a young rajah', 'trying to forget something very sad that had happened to me long ago', 'I tried very hard to die, but I seemed to bear an enchanted life' (p. 64). Gatsby lacks the vocabulary to express his thoughts, telling Daisy 'I keep it always full of interesting people, night and day. People who do interesting things. Celebrated people' (p. 87). Fitzgerald uses **aposiopesis** to make him sound inarticulate, for instance, when Daisy uses his hairbrush, he says to Nick, 'It's the funniest thing, old sport...I can't — When I try to —' (p. 89).

We may admire Gatsby for being a faithful lover, even after the object of his love marries someone else; he chivalrously intends to take the blame when Daisy kills Myrtle, and he keeps a sacred 'vigil' that

Context

Gatsby's defining expression, 'old sport', was first used in 1905. Fitzgerald saved a note from a Long Island bootlegger named von Gerlach, written on a newspaper photo of the Fitzgeralds, saying 'How are you and the family, Old Sport?'

aposiopesis
incomplete utterance caused by emotion or confusion

night to protect Daisy. However, Fitzgerald may be calling him 'Great' ironically, linking him with circus performers and showmen who advertised their acts as 'Great'. It is surely ironic that the one chivalrous character in the novel is engaged in business that is intended to cheat and defraud.

Nick Carraway

Nick Carraway (aged 29) is the novel's narrator and we see all the other characters from his point of view. He was brought up in the Midwest, but his family is prosperous and his father is funding his year in New York. He graduated from Yale University and fought in the Great War. When he returned, his horizons had been broadened, and he could not settle back into a place with such a narrow perspective on life. He went east to New York to learn how to make his fortune in the bond business. He rents a cottage on West Egg, next to Gatsby's mansion, and he makes it possible for Gatsby to meet Daisy, who is Nick's cousin. Nick dreams of romance, but is unable to commit himself, and seems to have settled for a dream of wealth.

Nick has had a puritanical upbringing that has erroneously taught him that 'a sense of the fundamental decencies is parcelled out unequally at birth', so, in spite of boasting of his tolerance, he is quick to judge others. However, it is interesting that a man who claims to be one of the few honest people he has ever known thinks that being asked to help Gatsby to seduce another man's wife is a 'modest' demand, 'such a little thing'. It seems that his romantic soul thinks love excuses everything. When he phones Daisy, he tells her not to bring Tom, so he is not merely a bystander but complicit in the seduction. In order to give Gatsby and Daisy privacy, Nick not only leaves the room but goes and stands outside in the rain for half an hour.

Fitzgerald gives his narrator a distinctive voice, using the Latinate vocabulary one might expect from a graduate of Yale, but also using colloquial language that conveys informality; we often feel he is talking to us rather than crafting a book. However, he rarely uses sophisticated polysyllabic words in speech. He uses colloquialisms and occasionally swearwords to express intense emotion. He is also able to slip easily into Daisy's hyperbolic and inconsequential style of chatter, e.g. 'The whole town is desolate' (p. 15). However, he is forthright in his criticism: 'You're a rotten driver,' he protests, 'Either you ought to be more careful, or you oughtn't to drive at all' (p. 59).

> *Pause for **Thought***
>
> If you have watched one of the film versions, discuss how faithfully Nick has been presented.

Daisy Buchanan (née Fay)

Context

Louisville is in Kentucky, one of the Southern States. Scottie, Fitzgerald's daughter, criticised Mia Farrow's portrayal of Daisy in the 1974 film because she did not convey the 'intensely Southern' nature of Daisy's character.

The derivation of the flower's name is from the phrase 'day's eye' and Daisy certainly glows like the sun. However, a daisy is a surprising flower to choose as the name for this rich, sophisticated woman. It does not suggest wealth or even beauty, but perhaps Fitzgerald wished to suggest that she retained a pure, unaffected innocence underneath her cynicism. She is still the nice girl who grew up in Louisville, immaculately dressed in white and lamenting her white girlhood. 'Fay' is an archaic word for fairy, and Gatsby's perception of Daisy is one of enchantment. He is 'consumed with wonder at her presence' (p. 89), and, when he first kissed her, 'At his lips' touch she blossomed for him like a flower and the incarnation was complete' (p. 107).

However, in the Arthurian legends, Morgan le Fay is a seductive sorceress who uses her magical powers to try to overthrow King Arthur. Daisy Fay's name encapsulates the enigma of the character, and readers are left to make up their own minds whether she is the innocent girl of Gatsby's dream, or a seductive sorceress, using him and then betraying him.

In a letter to his publisher, Maxwell Perkins, Fitzgerald wrote: 'I'm sorry Myrtle is better than Daisy....It's chapter VII that's the trouble with Daisy and it may hurt the book's popularity that it's *a man's book*.' In another letter, he wrote, 'the book contains no important woman character,' and it is true that none of the women is ever given a voice. Our impression of them is always filtered through Nick's negative perception. Daisy remains shadowy because she is not allowed to tell her own story.

In the novel's present, Daisy is 23, disillusioned and unhappy because of her husband's infidelity. However, she hides her feelings behind a mask of shallow cynicism. Just a few years earlier she had been the 'golden girl' (p. 115) with everything before her, but now, thanks to Tom's 'little spree' in Chicago, she is living in relative isolation in East Egg.

Pause for *Thought*

How have the additional scenes in the 1974 film affected our feelings about Daisy and Tom?

Daisy stutters a little, suggesting helplessness, and uses hyperbole, 'I'm p-paralysed with happiness'. She uses a lot of short questions, exclamations, empty adjectives such as 'gorgeous' and 'absolute' and tells empty stories like the one about the butler's nose (p. 19). She appears to be talking to be sociable and create a light-hearted atmosphere, not because she has anything meaningful to say. This is emphasised when, over dinner, she and Jordan talk 'unobtrusively and with a bantering inconsequence that was never quite chatter' (p. 17). When she is alone with Nick, she uses a more direct style of speech as she tries to confide in him, but he is unreceptive, assuming that she is still indulging in insincere chatter.

Tom Buchanan

Tom's immense wealth is inherited, so it places him socially, like Daisy, in the old-established 'aristocracy'. By saying that his wealth was made in Chicago, Fitzgerald links Tom with ruthless exploitation as Chicago had a notorious meat-packing industry with an appalling record of exploiting the workers. He was educated at Yale University, where he distinguished himself on the football field, and he still has the physique of an American football player. He is now a well-known polo player and his muscles strain against the riding clothes he wears. Like his clothes, his veneer of civilised behaviour has difficulty keeping his strength under control. He is domineering, aggressive and arrogant.

Tom has had a succession of affairs since his marriage three years before the novel opens and is keen to show off his current mistress, but he is blatantly hypocritical, being outraged at Daisy's relationship with Gatsby. The most unpleasant thing about him is his self-righteousness and self-absorption. Tom has a hierarchical view of society with him and his ilk at the top and he violently disapproves of anything that threatens his superiority. He is an extreme racist, although Nick observes that he does not have the intelligence to understand the book he has been reading, and he disapproves of women having too much freedom.

Tom feels quite justified in giving Wilson directions to Gatsby's house, even though he admits to knowing that Wilson has a gun. Although he claims the moral high ground in the confrontation with Gatsby, he is not untouched by corruption himself. He is friendly with Walter Chase (one of Wolfshiem's and Gatsby's criminal associates), he frequents speakeasies, like the one in the cellar on Forty-Second Street, he buys alcohol illegally and even smuggles it into the Plaza Hotel. Tom is both amoral and ruthless.

Tom's first word is the first person singular subject pronoun. The declaration he makes, 'I've got a nice place here', excludes his wife, suggesting egocentrism and arrogance. He speaks assertively and 'violently' (e.g. 'Civilization's going to pieces'), but his authority is undermined by his use of vague, basic speaking vocabulary (e.g. 'It's all scientific stuff' and 'science and art, and all that'). He speaks aggressively, using swear words ('God damned fool'), and he violates the rules of turn-taking by interrupting both Daisy and Jordan.

Context

Upton Sinclair exposed corruption in the Chicago meat-packing industry in his novel *The Jungle*. Ironically, instead of horrifying people at the situation of the workers, who sometimes fell into the meat-processing tanks and were ground up along with the meat, his novel evoked an outcry against the lack of food safety measures, highlighting even further the hypocrisy of society.

Context

Speakeasies sold alcohol during Prohibition, when the sale, manufacture and transportation of alcohol were illegal. The term comes from a patron's manner of ordering alcohol without raising suspicion — a bartender would tell a patron to be quiet and 'speak easy'.

Jordan Baker

Jordan knew Daisy in Louisville, and she forcibly persuaded Daisy to marry Tom when she wanted to change her mind. Nick describes her as slender, boyish, 'like a young cadet', her eyes 'sun-strained', her face 'wan, charming, discontented', and 'there was a jauntiness about her movements as if she had first learned to walk upon golf courses on clean crisp mornings' (pp. 51–52).

Context

The Professional Golfers' Association was formed in 1916. Fitzgerald modelled Jordan Baker on the golfer Edith Cummings, the winner of the 1923 US Women's Amateur Golf Championship, whom he met at Princeton University in 1915 (although there was no suggestion that Cummings cheated). Cummings turned professional after her 1923 win.

Jordan is a successful professional golfer, a well-known sports celebrity whose 'pleasing contemptuous expression had looked out… from many rotogravure pictures of the sporting life' (p. 23). She is also the target of nasty gossip, making accusations that she cheats. She is pursued by young men who expect her to fall into their arms, attracted to her because of her sporting success and her good looks. Jordan's parents are dead, and she lives with an elderly aunt, so she has had to learn to look out for herself. As a defence, she has adopted a pose of contemptuous cynicism and self-sufficiency. Nick calls her a 'clean, hard, limited person, who dealt in universal scepticism' (p. 77).

At 21, she is Daisy's close friend and thinks 'Daisy ought to have something in her life'. This is why she persuades Nick to invite Daisy to his bungalow to meet Gatsby. Unlike Daisy, Jordan says very little and weighs her words carefully. Jordan can engage in sociable bantering like Daisy, but she usually adopts a more assertive manner of speaking, reflecting her independent, sporty image: 'I don't give a damn about you now' (p. 168). Her first word, 'Absolutely', expresses a vehement agreement that Tom should stay in the East. Whereas Daisy uses the adjectival form without meaning in phrases like 'an absolute rose', Jordan uses the adverb to be assertive. Her first words to Nick, 'You live in West Egg', are a declarative statement, issued rather like a challenge. Since he is not used to forthright women, he interprets her tone as contemptuous.

Myrtle Wilson

Named after a hardy evergreen shrub that was sacred to Aphrodite, Greek goddess of love, Myrtle is Tom's current lover. She is vigorous and manages to retain her lust for life: 'there was an immediately perceptible vitality about her as if the nerves of her body were continually smouldering' (p. 28). This vitality refuses to let her give up as her husband has, and it makes her grasp at the chance to lift herself out of the valley of ashes.

Like Gatsby, Myrtle has a strong dream but she can achieve it only through a man. With Tom's money, she sets up a town establishment and apes the rich. Having, as she thinks, lifted herself out of the spiritless, hopeless environs of the valley of ashes, she despises her husband and speaks with contempt of her own class, evincing 'despair at the shiftlessness of the lower orders' (p. 34). However, her dream is built on a lie. Tom claims that the only reason he cannot marry her is because Daisy is Catholic, which she is not. Tom exploits her version of the American Dream by leading her on, just as he leads her husband on to hope that he will let him have the car, just to give him an excuse to go to the garage.

Nick employs non-standard orthography to mock Myrtle's lower-class accent with 'you'd of thought' and 'fellas'. He combines this with vocabulary errors such as the misspelt 'appendicitus' instead of 'appendix' to mock her lack of education. This undermines her pretensions. She uses clumsy grammatical constructions like the multiple negative, 'I didn't hardly know I wasn't getting into a subway train' (p. 38). She also uses basic speaking vocabulary with no auxiliary verbs, 'I got to write down a list so I won't forget all the things I got to do'.

George Wilson

Myrtle's husband runs a garage, but the car in it is wrecked and covered in dust, suggesting he is too tired to work, or even to dream. Nick describes Wilson as a 'blond, spiritless man, anaemic, and faintly handsome' (pp. 27–28). He was 'one of these worn-out men: when he wasn't working, he sat on a chair in the doorway and stared at the people and cars…He was his wife's man and not his own' (p. 130). Michaelis 'was almost sure that Wilson had no friend: there was not enough of him for his wife' (p. 151). However, when he learns about Myrtle's affair, Wilson locks her in and sets about finding the money to take her west. When she is killed, he is distraught, but about 12 hours later he walks about 20 miles to find the driver of the car that killed her.

At the inquest, it is assumed that Wilson shot Gatsby and then himself because he was 'deranged by grief'. Wilson is misled into thinking that Gatsby killed Myrtle because she was hit by his car and that Gatsby was her lover because she recognised the car and ran out to speak to the driver. However, it seems unlikely that a man as poor as Wilson would own a gun. Fitzgerald eliminates the possibility that he might have served in the Great War, so it would have been difficult for him to acquire the marksmanship needed to kill Gatsby outright as he floated on an airbed on the pool, without puncturing the mattress.

*Pause for **Thought***

How close to the truth do you think the verdict of the inquest was?

Wilson's lack of education is revealed in his accent, 'How could she of been like that?', his basic speaking vocabulary, 'got', 'funny', 'nice', 'get', and his non-standard grammar, as when he uses the adjective 'wise' colloquially as a verb in 'I just got wised up to something funny' (p. 118). He uses few bisyllabic or polysyllabic words and those are simple ones.

Meyer Wolfshiem

Context

In the infamous Black Sox Scandal of 1919, some members of the Chicago White Sox baseball team accepted bribes to lose games so that the Cincinnati Reds would win.

Wolfshiem is a professional gambler, the man who, according to Gatsby, fixed the 1919 Baseball World Series. Based on the real-life Arnold Rothstein (see p. 68 of this guide), he is involved in a range of other illegal activities including importing and selling alcohol. As his name suggests, he is a ruthless man, although Nick's mocking anti-Semitism means that Wolfshiem actually comes across as a comic character with his 'tragic nose' and his 'business gonnegtion'. He recruited Gatsby when the latter returned from the war and it is presumably to him that Gatsby owes his wealth. Wolfshiem has an apparently respectable office on Broadway marked 'The Swastika Holding Company'.

Even before the Nazis took it over in 1920, the swastika had been in use as a symbol of German nationalist movements. It is difficult to believe that, by 1922, a Jew would not know that Hitler had adopted this device. Hitler was making no secret of his anti-Semitism, so this could be a cleverly ironic front to mask Wolfshiem's criminal activities.

Taking it Further

Watch *Eight Men Out*, the 1988 film based on the Black Sox Scandal.

Wolfshiem has a distinctive nasal east European accent, using the nasal velar plosive /g/ instead of /k/. Like Myrtle, he uses 'of' instead of 'have' and non-standard grammar such as 'It was six of us' (p. 68), 'He hadn't eat anything for a couple of days' and 'I knew I could use him good' (p. 162). Sometimes he speaks like a gangster with a controlling directness: 'I said "All right, Katspaugh, don't pay him a penny till he shuts his mouth." He shut it then and there' (p. 68). Sometimes he masks his profession by using the first person plural imperative form like a clergyman: 'Let us learn to show our friendship for a man when he is alive and not after he is dead' (p. 163).

Michaelis

Nick is not present when Myrtle is killed, so Fitzgerald uses the evidence Michaelis gives to the inquest to fill in the gaps. This Greek immigrant, who has run the 'coffee joint beside the ash-heaps' for four years, seems to be a good neighbour and a reliable witness. After Myrtle's death, he stays with Wilson until dawn, trying to distract him from his grief.

Form, structure and language

There are numerous points made about Fitzgerald's choices of form, structure and language in the chapter commentaries, so this section will focus on particular aspects.

Form

Unreliable narrator

In a first-person narrative, an understanding of the character selected to put his or her version of events is crucial to an understanding of the whole novel. When the narrator is a character involved in events as well as commenting on them, readers should be alert and prepared to question the accuracy of the account. Nick has a vivid imagination that he uses to interpret people's reactions and feelings, but this makes him gullible, so Fitzgerald can gloss over the means by which Gatsby became rich and concentrate on his dream. Nick actually admits to misleading his readers when he quotes the butler's words and then retracts them, saying: 'What he really said was...' (p. 10).

> ...readers should be prepared to question the accuracy of Nick's account

Furthermore, Nick has had limited experience of life, which may lead him to misinterpret events. He has had a puritanical upbringing that has shaped his prejudices and opinions, erroneously teaching him that 'a sense of the fundamental decencies is parcelled out unequally at birth' (p. 7), so, in spite of boasting of his tolerance, he is quick to judge others. Nick's upbringing allows Fitzgerald to reveal his own feelings about the hollowness of the lives of the postwar generation. Nick also prides himself on having been 'rather literary in college', so he shapes his narrative, being selective in what he chooses to include and to omit. Fitzgerald provides evidence that he is carefully constructing his narrative. Nick tells us that he is writing a 'book' whose title includes Gatsby's name (p. 8); he pauses to read through what he has written so far and correct false impressions (p. 56), and he defends a narrative choice to deviate from his plan of unfolding events as he experienced

them and to give us some of Gatsby's account of his early life (p. 97). Nick again presents something out of sequence and explains why (p. 148) and the final chapter is Nick's own story of the aftermath of Gatsby's death.

Fitzgerald has chosen to modify the narrative and employ a narrator who is only partially involved. At times he relies on the testimony of other characters. However, Nick's unreliability leads us to question his account of what he claims others have told him, so different interpretations of events are possible. This means that key scenes of the story can be left to the reader's imagination, thus enhancing the mystery. Fitzgerald's choice of narrator allows us to glimpse the glory of Gatsby's illusion and simultaneously makes us aware of its hopelessness by keeping us in touch with reality.

*Pause for **Thought***

Discuss the problems posed for a film director by the use of an involved narrator. Explore how one (or more) of the film versions has dealt with this problem.

Structure

Modifying the narrative

Fitzgerald uses Nick as a framing device to help hold the novel together. The first few pages introduce him, and the final chapter is the story of what happened to him after Gatsby's death. Nick supposedly selects what to include in his book and tells us what he remembers that others have told him.

Context

Fitzgerald wrote in a letter in 1925: 'The worst fault in [*The Great Gatsby*] I think is a BIG FAULT: I gave no account (and had no feeling about or knowledge of) the emotional relations between Gatsby and Daisy from the time of their reunion to the catastrophe.'

Jordan Baker tells what she knows about the early relationship between Gatsby and Daisy, and this is supposedly written in her own words (pp. 72–76). Fitzgerald juxtaposes Gatsby's present with his past by cutting dramatically from the scene where we have been introduced to Gatsby's criminal activities to Jordan's first words. He then breaks off to tell us, in parenthesis, that she was 'sitting up very straight on a straight chair'. The repetition of 'straight' seems to suggest that her account will be 'straight' also, unembellished by her imagination. This technique makes her account credible but leaves Daisy's thoughts and feelings a mystery.

By contrast, when Gatsby tells his story (pp. 106–07), Nick breaks off the dialogue to put it in his own words. Gatsby is not well educated and not very articulate, as revealed in the childlike language with which he asserts: 'I'm going to fix everything just the way it was before… She'll see.' Nick tells his readers that he found Gatsby's sentimentality 'appalling', and so he turns the account into a romantic quest. Fitzgerald planned to write a tragic novel — he wanted to create a quality of 'hauntedness'. It is only by giving Gatsby's story to another that he was able to achieve this.

The rest of Gatsby's story is told on pp. 141–46. Once again Nick takes control and interprets the story according to his own imagination. If Fitzgerald had used Gatsby to tell his story in his own words, his manner of speaking would have made it very prosaic and undermined the title of the novel.

Because Nick did not witness Myrtle's death, the details of the accident are recounted factually, as told at the inquest and written up in the newspapers, but Nick has supposedly reconstructed events as a connected narrative.

Task **8**

Compare Gatsby's account of his first kiss with Daisy (p. 143) with Nick's interpretation (p. 107).

Arousing the audience's interest in Gatsby

In the first three chapters our interest in Gatsby is aroused in a number of ways. A passing comment by Jordan is picked up by Daisy, who mysteriously demands to know more about him. In Chapter III, Nick gives a detailed description of Gatsby's parties from the perspective of a neighbouring observer, using the present tense to give immediacy, then a description of one particular party he attended as a guest, given in the past tense.

At the party the guests gossip about Gatsby, discussing the various rumours. They whisper and look round for Gatsby as if afraid of him. Dramatically, Fitzgerald uses body language to create suspense as the girl who said that he killed a man 'leaned forward with enthusiasm' then 'narrowed her eyes and shivered'. When Nick meets him, he is unaware of Gatsby's identity, so we are given an unbiased, denotative description: 'a man of about my age' who speaks 'politely' and recognises Nick from the war in France. Nick takes little notice of Gatsby until he learns his identity, and then his description is vivid and detailed.

After the party, Fitzgerald employs a cinematic technique, giving us a long-distance shot of Gatsby mysteriously trembling as he stretches out his arms towards the dark water and a single green light.

How Fitzgerald condenses information

The events of the story cover some 18 years, from when Gatsby wrote his schedule in September 1906, before leaving home and meeting Dan Cody in 1907, to when Nick supposedly finished writing his book in 1924. However, instead of a long-drawn-out story, Fitzgerald concentrates

on just four months, fracturing Nick's narrative with accounts of past events told by different characters.

Fitzgerald also condenses information in other ways. A summary of Nick's routine life in New York gives a realistic touch and valuable insights into the narrator's personality without extending the novel unnecessarily (pp. 56–58). The list of names written on a timetable is another way in which Fitzgerald gives the impression of historical fact but also imaginatively evokes an impression of a continuous sequence of parties attended by large numbers of people (pp. 60–61). At the same time, the passing references suggest private tragedies which reveal that, although this generation may appear carefree, its pursuit of the American Dream is doomed to failure. References to sudden death (Doctor Webster Civet), prison (Snell), murder (Muldoon), corruption (Ferret), suicide (Henry L. Palmetto) and war injury (Brewer) all combine to give an impression of people seeking to drown their sorrows, and suggest that Gatsby's tragedy is not exceptional.

By condensing *The Great Gatsby* into a few short months, the emotion is intensified and the book becomes a psychological drama being played out within Nick's imagination rather than a consecutive series of events. Nick recognises in Gatsby's story his own poignant realisation that what he 'had almost remembered was uncommunicable forever' (p. 107). Both Nick and Gatsby think that, at some elusive point in the past, they could have achieved an ideal self, but that time has gone and, in reality, it never existed.

Non-linear narrative structure

The critic James E. Miller Jr plots the sequence of events in *The Great Gatsby* in this way: 'Allowing X to stand for the straight chronological account of the summer of 1922, and A, B, C, D, and E to represent the significant events of Gatsby's past, the nine chapters of *The Great Gatsby* may be charted: X, X, X, XCX, X, XBXCX, X, XCXDXD, XEXAX.'

This clearly shows how Fitzgerald planned his novel. For the most part, we are given information in the order in which Nick gets it, as we might learn about a new acquaintance in real life. Our interest is aroused in Gatsby through hints and rumours before we meet him; we learn nothing about his past until we have met the man himself. Even then his past is an enigma as Gatsby gives Nick contradictory information. We actually learn more about Nick's feelings about Gatsby than we do about the man himself, because he never tells his own story — Nick interprets for him.

Task 9

What questions in the novel about the characters and their behaviour does Fitzgerald leave open to the reader's interpretation?

The material included in this novel is highly selective. Fitzgerald uses the scenic method of narrative construction, which he admired in the novels of Henry James and Edith Wharton, but he does not tell us much about what happens between these scenes. We know only what Nick finds out, and we have to piece the story together from the details he supposedly remembers, being aware all the time that his interpretation is not necessarily the one Fitzgerald wants us to adopt. The scenes that Nick can describe at first hand are either ones where he hears one person's account of events or social gatherings at which Nick is present. Although the scenes are separate and self-contained, Fitzgerald does more than link them as different scenes in the story. He creates intricate patterns of imagery and symbolism, and some of the scenes parallel or contrast with others. For instance:

- In Chapter I, Daisy and Tom hold a dinner party for Jordan and Nick; the 'fifth guest' (p. 21) is the telephone, bringing Tom's 'other woman' as an intruder. In Chapter VII, Daisy and Tom hold a luncheon party. This time the fifth guest is Gatsby.

- In Chapters III, IV and VI, 'the world and its mistress' flock to Gatsby's parties. In Chapter IX, Gatsby's funeral is attended by the postman, four or five servants, his father and only two of the guests who had come to his parties.

Language

Names

We have already explored the significance of the names of the women characters. Fitzgerald has also made up names for the guests at Gatsby's parties. The list Nick supposedly wrote on a timetable is a deliberately comic addition to the novel in which Fitzgerald enjoys himself with puns and satirical wordplay. He gives people names of plants (Hornbeam, Endive, Orchid, Duckweed), of land animals (Civet, Blackbuck, Beaver, Klipspringer), of marine animals (Whitebait, Hammerhead, Beluga). Since he has chosen appropriate plant names for Daisy and Myrtle, we can assume he wishes us to attribute to the guests the characteristics of the various plants and animals. When we meet Klipspringer, for instance, in Chapter V, he is nervous and jumpy, like a small antelope.

Fitzgerald's use of names reflects the metaphor of a 'melting pot' or crucible to describe the process of immigration and colonisation by

Task 10

Draw a flow-chart to trace how Fitzgerald uses the seasons as a structuring device in the novel, and uses the weather to reflect or enhance the mood.

❮ Top ten *quotation*

Fitzgerald's use of names reflects the metaphor of a 'melting pot'

which different nationalities, cultures and races were to blend into a new utopian community. He uses Irish names (Mulready, Muldoon), Germanic and east European (Schoen, Gulick), Mediterranean (Legros) as well as Jewish (Cohen). However, none of the guests are Native Americans and none come from Asia or Africa.

Symbolism

In literature, a symbol combines an image with a concept and represents something more than itself. Whenever we read a literary text, we bring our previous experience with us, so a writer knows that images will evoke particular associations. When Fitzgerald uses imagery, he expects us to have ideas about what these images represent. When the same or similar images are used frequently throughout the novel, they achieve a particular resonance and increase in power.

The green light

Green represents new life, youth and hope, but also inexperience and naivety. Green stands for grass, growth, and the natural landscape of newly discovered territory. Travellers are given the green light as a signal that they can move forward. We bring these associations to our response to the green light at the end of Daisy's dock, but it gradually achieves a special significance.

Fitzgerald suggests that the green light is like a religious icon to Gatsby as he stretches out his arms towards it (p. 25). To Gatsby the green light might offer encouragement, but the reader may feel that green suggests the naivety of his dream that he can recreate the past, that Daisy will declare that she never loved Tom. Gatsby mentions the light to Daisy (p. 90) and Nick notes that 'Possibly it had occurred to him that the colossal significance of that light had now vanished forever.' Nick suggests that the inaccessibility of his dream was what turned the green light into 'an enchanted object'.

Top ten *quotation* ❯

Top ten *quotation* ❯

Nick says that 'Gatsby believed in the green light, the orgastic future that year by year recedes before us' (p. 171), suggesting that it represented the orgasm, the intensity of experience that is forever beyond reach. Just before this reference, Nick was imagining how the Dutch sailors felt when they first arrived in America and saw 'a fresh, green breast of the new world. Its vanished trees…had once pandered in whispers to the last and greatest of all human dreams'. By juxtaposing the green breast and the green light, Fitzgerald makes the green light a symbol of the

American Dream, rooted in the past, but forever out of reach. Those who pursue it do so at the expense of the values of a caring society. Those who seem to have achieved it are living in a moral vacuum that destroys any hope of happiness. Significantly, the green light, which had seemed to symbolise an invitation to Gatsby to go ahead and to suggest the hope of a new life with Daisy, lured Gatsby to his death.

Images of vision and insight

Dr T. J. Eckleburg

Fitzgerald makes many references to eyes in the novel; the most haunting are those which stare out of a huge billboard placed next to the railway line in the valley of ashes to attract travellers' attention. Each time Fitzgerald's characters go to town, 'the giant eyes of Doctor T. J. Eckleburg kept their vigil' (p. 118). Wilson takes Myrtle to the window to see the eyes and says 'God knows what you've been doing…You may fool me, but you can't fool God.' (p. 152). He assumes the eyes see everything, but these eyes are blind. Perhaps Fitzgerald, who was brought up as a Catholic but left the Church in 1917, is saying that there is no God watching over us.

The eyes are 'dimmed a little by many paintless days' (p. 26), just as people's spirituality has been dimmed by neglect. The 'wild wag of an oculist' placed the advertisement to 'fatten his practice' in one of the affluent areas of New York, but he has moved on. This uncaring materialistic society abandons the poor when it becomes clear that there is no money to be made. Society suffers from 'eternal blindness' or from forgetfulness. Perhaps we are meant to think of God as a 'wild wag' who watches us making fools of ourselves and losing that clarity of vision needed to live by moral precepts. Fitzgerald's God, like the oculist, is merely absent, or mocking us for our failures.

On the other hand, Nick personifies the eyes as 'brooding' over the solemn dumping ground, suggesting that the presence they represent is disappointed by people's behaviour. Perhaps Fitzgerald is using the eyes to suggest a presence, whom some call God, that is watching over society all the time and will hold us accountable for our actions, even if we do fool the people around us. It seems to be an ironic comment that, in a consumer society, dreams of owning material possessions have replaced spiritual values, or perhaps a reminder that people's vision needs correcting so that they can appreciate the things that really matter.

…people's vision needs correcting

'Owl Eyes'

In the mythology of ancient Greece, Athene, goddess of wisdom, was so impressed by the great eyes and solemn appearance of the owl that she honoured the night bird by making him her favourite. It was believed that a magical 'inner light' gave owls night vision. The owl was a protector, accompanying Greek armies to war, and it also kept a watchful eye on Athenian trade and commerce from the reverse side of their coins. By using this childish nickname for one of Gatsby's guests, Fitzgerald suggests that he also has vision and insight.

Owl Eyes sees past Gatsby's assumed persona and realises that, although the books are real, Gatsby has not read any of them. He mutters that 'if one brick was removed the whole library was liable to collapse' (p. 47), a hyperbolic statement which recognises that Gatsby's dream is founded 'on a fairy's wing' (p. 96). However, he is not interested in the content of the books, and he is not interested in Gatsby's reason for creating the illusion. He is content to be impressed by Gatsby's skills at stage-management. He has blinkered vision.

Top ten *quotation* ❭

Owl Eyes is the only one of Gatsby's party guests to attend his funeral. The rain obscures his vision, and he has to remove his glasses to wipe them. However, he is the only one to say 'Amen' to the murmur 'Blessed are the dead that the rain fall on', and he calls on his God to witness his shock that none of Gatsby's other visitors have come to the funeral. He may have defective vision, but perhaps it is his 'inner light' which gives him the most compassionate line in the novel: 'The poor son-of-a-bitch'.

Nick Carraway as observer

Nick is our eyes; we see only what he notices and comments on. As we saw when discussing the theme of appearance and reality, he is not an omniscient narrator but filters the reader's view of events through his own insight or lack of it. Nick is, by nature, an onlooker, and examples of this are given in the *Themes* section (see pp. 30–31 of this guide).

After Myrtle's death Nick spies on Tom and Daisy through the window, like a voyeur, and, because he senses intimacy between them, his final comment is that Gatsby is 'watching over nothing' (p. 139). After Gatsby's death, Nick realises that 'the East was haunted for me..., distorted beyond my eyes' power of correction' (p. 167), reminding the reader once again that we are reading Nick's interpretation of characters and events, filtered through his defective vision.

Task *11*

How has one of the film versions used Fitzgerald's images? Where and why have new images been created for the film?

Finally, sprawled on the beach, Nick broods 'on the old unknown world', seeing through the eyes of the Dutch sailors who first arrived in America.

Cars

Cars have an important symbolic function in the novel and are associated with particular characters.

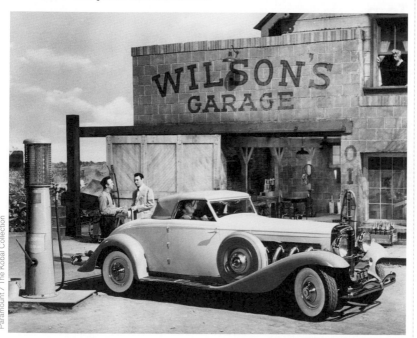

Paramount / The Kobal Collection

A still from a 1949 film version showing Gatsby's car outside Wilson's garage. Tom is talking to Wilson, and Myrtle sees him from the window

Gatsby

For young Gatsby, Daisy's house became a centre of romance, mystery and wealth, 'redolent of this year's shining motor cars' (p. 141). For him, cars are a symbol of wealth and power. Gatsby drives an amazing car that Tom refers to as 'a circus wagon' (p. 115). It is appropriate that Gatsby, the man who reinvented himself at 17, the man who builds his life on a dream, the man who turns his house into an imitation of the World's Fair, should have a car born of the fantastic dreams of a teenager. He shows it off to Nick with typical understatement: 'It's pretty, isn't it, old sport?' (p. 63). The car, however, is not merely a symbol of his wealth; it is an outlet for his restlessness. 'He was never quite still' (p. 63) and he takes Nick on a reckless detour through Astoria, until they attract the attention of the police.

...the car is an outlet for Gatsby's restlessness

Daisy

In her youth, Daisy had a 'little white roadster' (p. 63), which gave her the freedom to lead an independent life. As a married woman, she has a chauffeur who appears critical of her visiting Nick at West Egg,

suggesting that she may be under supervision. Daisy's attempt to have a glamorous affair, losing her nerve at the confrontation, is symbolised by her attempt to drive Gatsby's car at speed.

Tom

Tom usually travels to New York by train, so that Myrtle can join him without arousing suspicion. His car gives him an excuse to go to her husband's garage, and he keeps Wilson sweet by promising to sell it to him. Wilson refers to it as an 'old car' (p. 117), so clearly Tom does not regard it as a status symbol. Tom is a careless driver and, just after his return from his honeymoon, he 'ran into a wagon on the Ventura road one night, and ripped a front wheel off his car' (p. 75). He races Gatsby (p. 119), and he is excited by the prospect of the crash, before he realises that Myrtle is dead (p. 131). A car gives Tom the freedom to have affairs, but it is something he finds useful rather than something he values.

Wilson

Cars are Wilson's livelihood, but he does not own a car and has to walk when he sets out to avenge Myrtle's death. The only car in his garage is covered in dust, which suggests he neglects his business. However, when Wilson finds out that Myrtle is having an affair, he dreams of selling a car to get the money to take her west (p. 118), so for him the car offers the only hope he has of earning enough to leave the valley of ashes.

Jordan Baker

Jordan's name is composed of two American makes of car, reflecting her modern image. She drives recklessly, carelessly flicking a button on the coat of a workman (p. 59). Her attitude is that other people should keep out of her way. The car represents her independence, but also the careless attitude of the rich. A curious conversation about driving between Nick and Jordan is actually about morality (p. 59). She accuses Nick of being another bad driver (p. 168), explaining that she was wrong in thinking him to be an honest, straightforward person.

References to accidents involving cars

Five references to accidents involving cars build up to the climax of Myrtle's violent death, so, although cars represent mobility and independence, in this novel they become a powerful symbol of the carelessness of the rich. They also symbolise the hopelessness of the poor, who can only dream of owning a car and going west. They are

> **Context**
>
> Thanks to the invention of production-line manufacturing, by 1914 an assembly-line worker could buy a Model T Ford with four months' pay.

…cars are a powerful symbol of the carelessness of the rich

used as symbols of wealth and power, but they also represent the restlessness of the postwar generation.

Patterns of imagery

In this novel, Fitzgerald is concerned to show how Gatsby managed to cherish a dream, to keep alive an idealised vision of Daisy, in a society where money and possessions define a person's value rather than their moral worth or their capacity for love. Fitzgerald uses imagery to convey the freshness and innocence of Nick's romantic appreciation of New York and of Gatsby's dream, and then contrasting imagery to convey the disillusionment as events unfold.

The future

Fitzgerald's use of imagery reveals a change in Nick's feelings about the future. A day or so after his arrival in West Egg, he declares: 'with the sunshine and the great bursts of leaves growing on trees, just as things grow in fast movies, I had that familiar conviction that life was beginning over again' (pp. 9–10). Here Fitzgerald offers a conventional romantic image of rebirth with trees bursting into leaf in the spring sunshine. However, he blends the natural image with a reference to the cinematic technique that speeds up the process. In this way, Fitzgerald manages to suggest Nick's enjoyment of the pace of life in the city, and that the future seemed exciting for a young man from the more rural Midwest.

> Fitzgerald… blends the natural image with a reference to the cinematic technique

Two or three months later, on his thirtieth birthday, after the confrontation in the Plaza Hotel, Fitzgerald reveals his disillusionment through his image of the future as a road that Nick personifies as 'menacing' (p. 129).

Recumbent women in white

Fitzgerald gives three images of women in white dresses at different points in the story, and his descriptions reflect his changing attitudes to New York.

- When Nick has recently arrived in New York, he describes Daisy and Jordan romantically as if they were fairies (or even angels) having just flown around the house (p. 13). The white dresses suggest that their 'white girlhood' (p. 24) has not left them and he thinks they are still pure and unsullied.

- The next time he sees Daisy and Jordan together, two or three months later, in a similar position, their dresses are still white (p. 110), but

Nick's disillusionment is revealed to the reader through Fitzgerald's subtle change of colour and imagery. The two young women no longer seem like spirits of the air, now they are 'like silver idols', materialistic and spiritually inert, weighing down their own dresses.

- After Gatsby is killed and Nick returns to the Midwest, his cynicism is revealed in the nightmares he has about West Egg (p. 167). This time the woman in white is drunk, lying on a stretcher, and her hand sparkles cold with jewels. 'No one knows the woman's name and no one cares.' Now, there is not even an illusion of warmth, life or friendship.

The heat and the sweat

Fitzgerald set the climax of his story on the hottest day of the year. The imagery Nick uses links the increasing tension to the heat. Fitzgerald uses synaesthesia, blending the senses of hearing and feeling to enhance the stifling atmosphere (p. 109). The 'hush' is described as 'simmering'; this metaphor compares the heat with a liquid, simmering on the stove, in danger of boiling over and scalding someone. The tension increases as they set off for town, and the heat is more intense. The gravel is like a 'blazing' fire, no longer threatening merely to scald, but to burn. By the time they reach the garage the tension increases because Wilson has found out that Myrtle is having an affair. Nick personifies the heat as unrelenting, having no compassion, and he feels physical pain as if he is being beaten (p. 118).

Once at the Plaza, Nick is no longer an onlooker; he is involved and feeling 'the heat and the sweat' (p. 120) in a very uncomfortable way. He is sweating profusely and his underpants are rolled up like a 'damp snake'. A snake has biblical connotations of betrayal, suggesting a subconscious guilt on Nick's part for his role in bringing Daisy and Gatsby together again. As Daisy rises to Gatsby's defence, the tension is so strong that 'The compressed heat exploded into sound'. It feels as if the hot air is compressed and stifling them. When the orchestra strikes up below, Fitzgerald once again employs synaesthesia to blend the senses of hearing and feeling so that it seems as if the tension explodes. This is the crisis point. The 'Wedding March' evokes shared memories of Tom's and Daisy's wedding, from which Gatsby is excluded. These give Tom the advantage so that Daisy no longer defends Gatsby by threatening to leave when Tom starts to goad Gatsby about Oxford.

Breasts and nurturing; birth and eggs

Fitzgerald also reveals changes in Nick's perception through references to breasts and nurturing, birth and eggs.

PHILIP ALLAN LITERATURE GUIDE **FOR A-LEVEL**

Eggs

When he first arrives in 'the great wet barnyard of Long Island Sound' in the spring (p. 10), Nick projects his own sense of wonder on to the gulls. His life is 'beginning all over again' and Fitzgerald's choice to change the landscape to resemble an egg suggests that it is appropriate for a place from which he hopes to hatch out into a 'well-rounded man'.

Birth

When Nick learns that Gatsby bought the house so that he would be near Daisy, he thinks he understands everything. An image of birth suggests this revelation, writing of Gatsby's 'purposeless splendour' as a womb from which he has emerged now that Nick knows why he has such an ostentatious lifestyle (p. 76). It is Gatsby's dream that makes him come alive for Nick.

By August, Nick has lost his sense of wonder and excitement. He thinks Daisy was 'appalled by West Egg, this unprecedented "place" that Broadway had begotten upon a Long Island fishing village'. Fitzgerald explains, by using an image of birth, that most of the residents of West Egg worked in the entertainment industry, suggesting that Broadway fertilised the egg and a community was born that was characterised by 'raw vigour' and which 'chafed under the old euphemisms' used by the inhabitants of East Egg.

Nurture

Nick imagines the turning point in Gatsby's life to be when he kissed Daisy (p. 107). Before that moment, in the moonlight, Gatsby felt that, alone, he could climb to a place where there was no limit to his aspirations, where life would feed his desires with the 'incomparable milk of wonder'. He knew that, once he kissed Daisy, she would become the incarnation of his dream, and, because she is human, with 'perishable breath', 'his mind would never romp again like the mind of God'. For this reason he hesitated before he lost this vision for ever and transferred his aspirations to Daisy. In this image, it is life that has the potential to nurture Gatsby's imagination, and the milk suggests he could return to a state of innocence.

Breasts

Nick's cynicism is revealed in his description of Daisy. He notices little details like the tiny gust of powder that rose from Daisy's bosom into the air when she laughed. Although she is a mother, her 'bosom' is not used for nurturing but is cosmetically enhanced as part of the image she creates to attract men (p. 110).

...Fitzgerald's choice to change the landscape to resemble an egg

It is Gatsby's dream that makes him come alive for Nick.

After the climactic scene in the Plaza Hotel, Nick has no illusions left. What he sees on the way back to East Egg is a brutal image of death. Myrtle's clothes are torn open to reveal a breast swinging loose like a flap. Myrtle's breast is not a symbol of motherhood but of her sexuality. The image he evokes blatantly carries the message that the sexuality with which she betrayed her husband has brought about her death (p. 110).

On the final page of the novel, Nick experiences for himself something of the vision that 'pandered in whispers to the last and greatest of all human dreams' (p. 171). Once again moonlight creates an illusion, and he can imagine what it must have been like to be one of the original settlers, seeing 'a fresh green breast' of Long Island with its two eggs, for the first time. It is America that promises 'the incomparable milk of wonder', and the American Dream is revived for Nick in spite of his close encounter with the reality.

Precious metals and jewellery

Fitzgerald also reveals Nick's attitudes in references to precious metals and jewellery. He imagines Gatsby like a romantic buccaneer, opening a chest of rubies (p. 65). The jewels are plunder, but in Nick's fantasy they have crimson hearts and console his hero's broken heart.

Nick's cynicism about Daisy is revealed in the way he specifies the amount of money Tom spent on Daisy's string of pearls, suggesting that he thinks Daisy is mercenary. Nick's fairy-tale description of Daisy as 'the golden girl' (p. 115) places her as an object of desire, out of reach because of her wealth; Nick is a romantic, but he is also aware of reality, and he interprets Daisy's charm as her inaccessibility. When Nick interprets how the young Lieutenant Gatsby had felt about Daisy, he uses a simile comparing her with 'silver, safe and proud above the hot struggles of the poor' (p. 142). This romantic description is once again tainted with the belief that Daisy's attraction lies in her wealth:

> **'Her voice is full of money,' he said suddenly.**
> **That was it. I'd never understood before. (p. 115)**

Nick's imagery reveals his attitude that Daisy is an object, 'silver', and the double meaning of 'safe' suggests that she is both protected by her wealth and inaccessible because of it.

The epigraph (p. 5) warns us in advance that Fitzgerald (or is it Nick?) intends us to see Daisy as shallow, attracted to Gatsby by his wealth and his showmanship. If she has no deep feelings for him, it is inevitable that she will let him down. His efforts to 'move her' are doomed to disappointment.

Juxtaposed ideas

Fitzgerald has deliberately juxtaposed certain ideas (that is, he has placed them next to each other) to achieve specific effects.

- 'They…drifted here and there unrestfully wherever people played polo and were rich together' (p. 11). The juxtaposition of playing a game and being rich is an ironic comment on the shallowness of those who do nothing useful either with their money or to earn it.

- 'men and girls came and went like moths among the whisperings and the champagne and the stars' (p. 41). The juxtaposition of 'whisperings' and 'champagne' with 'stars' emphasises by contrast the ephemeral quality of the people who flit like moths.

Oxymoron

Some of the juxtaposed ideas are apparently contradictory. 'Drifting' and 'unrestfully', for instance, seem to contradict each other, but actually Fitzgerald is highlighting the restlessness of the postwar generation and the aimlessness of their attempts to find things to do with their lives. Here are some other examples of oxymoron that Fitzgerald has used to achieve a particular effect.

- p. 69: 'ferocious delicacy': this oxymoron suggests that Wolfshiem's wolfish nature is always apparent, even when his manners are delicate. There is more to Wolfshiem than meets the eye.

- p. 95: 'ineffable gaudiness': this phrase sums up the contradiction in Gatsby, the 'great' man with the dream that is too glorious to put into words and 'Mr Nobody from Nowhere' with the tasteless house lit up 'like the World's Fair'.

Task 12

See if you can find more examples of apparently contradictory ideas.

Contexts

Biographical context

Fitzgerald

Francis Scott Fitzgerald emerged onto the literary stage just at the time that new technology was creating celebrities and, as with present-day stars, those, like him, who courted publicity often became victims of the media's insatiable appetite for 'news'. His early rise to stardom, his reckless celebrity lifestyle, his romantic but troubled marriage, his decline into alcoholism and premature death in 1940 have come to represent the spectacular boom and bust years of his era: the Roaring Twenties and the Great Depression.

At school and Princeton College, Fitzgerald put all his energies into writing lightweight stories and plays, but he struggled academically. He embraced new experiences with energy and enthusiasm, but always with that degree of detachment that enables a writer to collect material. He wrote, on his own admission, 'blindly, incessantly'. Fitzgerald was impetuous, energetic, a tease who liked to be teased. He drank a lot, but he liked to appear more drunk than he was and was not yet a habitual drinker.

In December 1915 he dropped out of Princeton temporarily. When he returned, Fitzgerald was able to look at his own failures with a detached eye and to see himself and others from a moral perspective. He turned away from humour and musical comedy to more serious writing. Like the Romantic poets, his perception of a writer was as someone who lives life intensely in order to write about his or her own feelings with a heightened perception.

While he was looking for intensity of experience to give depth to his writing, in 1917 America entered the First World War and Fitzgerald dropped out of university to enlist. He was sent for officer training, but although he desperately wanted to go to the war and always regretted the fact that he did not, he was unable to commit himself to anything other than writing.

Context

Fitzgerald did not take military training seriously. One day he put a hollow stove pipe into his knapsack to make it look heavy but feel light.

He was stationed at Camp Taylor, which is also where Gatsby goes for officer training.

Zelda

While at a camp in Alabama awaiting embarkation, he met Zelda Sayre, a kindred spirit with a similarly uninhibited and reckless love of life, with whom he fell passionately in love. She was from a socially prominent family, however, and she refused to marry Fitzgerald until he was a financial success. His first novel had been returned by the publishers, but Maxwell Perkins, an editor who would become very important to Fitzgerald, praised it for its originality and made concrete suggestions for improvements. Fitzgerald redrafted it, but it was turned down again, so, when he was discharged from the army in February 1919, he went to New York to make his fortune. Several months later he sold a story to a magazine for $30.

In June, Zelda broke off their engagement, so he went back to St Paul, Minnesota, to stay with his parents while he rewrote his novel. This time it was accepted, and Zelda agreed to marry him. Fitzgerald was already a divided soul. He wanted to write, but while he was writing he worried that he was missing out on living. He wanted to be a serious writer, but he also wanted to make a great deal of money. However, in 1920, it seemed he could have it all. In February he had a short story published in *The Saturday Evening Post* for a fee of $500; his novel was published in March and was well received, and he married the girl of his dreams in April.

Fitzgerald adored Zelda, but they had a very stormy relationship. She did not understand his ambition to be the best novelist of his generation, wanting him just to write short stories, as these brought in more money. He was always aware that she would not have married him without money, and that he might lose her. His second novel was published in March 1922, but it did not establish Fitzgerald as a major writer and did not earn enough money for him to give up writing for magazines. He had not, however, lost his ambition and, in September 1922, the couple rented a house near Great Neck, Long Island, 20 miles from New York City, and they embarked on a riotous year that provided the background for *The Great Gatsby*.

The Great Gatsby

Fitzgerald was determined that his next book should be different from and better than his previous two. Over the next two years, he wrote three short stories in which he prepared the ground for *The Great Gatsby*. 'Winter Dreams' and 'The Sensible Thing' are both about the loss

Taking it
Further

Do some research into Zelda and explore how far she provided the inspiration for Fitzgerald's presentation of Daisy. How valuable do you think it is to use a biographical approach to interpret a text?

The Granger Collection/TopFoto

of dreams, and 'Absolution' was originally intended as an early chapter of his novel, telling the story of Gatsby's childhood. The Great Gatsby was sent to the publishers in October 1924 and published in April 1925. The reviews were excellent and Fitzgerald received congratulatory letters from several eminent writers.

Fitzgerald later described the postwar years as 'the greatest, gaudiest spree in history', and he was its chronicler. In *The Great Gatsby* he captures the atmosphere of the Roaring Twenties when 'The whole golden boom was in the air — its splendid generosities, its outrageous corruptions, and the tortuous death struggle of the old America in prohibition' ('The Crack-Up', an autobiographical essay by Fitzgerald written in 1936). Fitzgerald was living the American Dream: he was young and good-

Francis Scott Fitzgerald, Zelda and their daughter 'Scottie', posing at Christmas

looking, and he had earned money and early success through his own hard work. However, he and Zelda were already partying wildly, drinking excessively and making exhibitions of themselves, just to get into the news. Fitzgerald himself acknowledged that he 'was pushed into the position not only of spokesman for the time but of the typical product of that same moment' ('The Crack-Up').

In many ways, *The Great Gatsby* is a product of Fitzgerald's attempts to confront his own conflicting feelings about the Jazz Age. He was seduced by the wild and extravagant life of the rich, and he wanted to be at the heart of it, like Gatsby, but he was also aware of the moral emptiness and the hypocrisy beneath the excitement.

Historical context

America

European settlers first arrived, in the sixteenth and seventeenth centuries, full of hope that they could leave behind the old country with its prejudices and hierarchy and forge a new life where hard work was the key to success. They found a fertile land that offered a dream of riches they had not even imagined when they left.

From the beginning, the American Dream has been contaminated by exploitation and a desire for profit. The pioneers pushed westward, partly out of the excitement of exploration and discovery, but also in the hope of wealth. The unknown interior, with huge tracts of fertile land awaiting claimants, represented their dream of a new life. Idealism and hope are essential ingredients of American history, but they have always gone hand in hand with the drive for material gain.

For Americans, the West has always been a powerful symbol of opportunity and freedom. Going west was always seen as following the path of the sun and therefore the setting in the west is the end of the trail and the pioneers' journeys, their hopes and dreams. However, life for the pioneers who pushed forward the frontier of civilisation in the Wild West was hard, and the law was difficult to enforce, so they developed a distinctive American spirit, very different from those who remained in the East, where the influence of the 'Old World' was stronger.

Even when the continent had been 'tamed', mineral deposits exploited and the West Coast populated, so that there were no longer so many opportunities to make one's fortune, the West remained a symbol of freedom. After the war, many Americans stayed in Europe or soon returned to the 'Old World' because they could not accept the old ways of provincial life at home. For others, the financial and business world on the Eastern Seaboard came to symbolise the opportunity to make lots of money quickly.

The American Dream

Although this term was not coined until the twentieth century, the concept has its roots in the American Declaration of Independence in 1776. The Founding Fathers of America set out their vision in the justification for breaking away from British rule:

> **We hold these Truths to be self-evident, that all men are created equal, that they are endowed by their Creator with certain unalienable Rights, that among these are Life, Liberty and the Pursuit of Happiness.**

Immigrants to America were escaping from oppressive government, from conflict, from resistance to progress, from poverty, and they saw America as a blank slate upon which they could create their vision of a perfect state, completely free from the inequalities of life in the Old World. They

Context

The Dutch West India Company sent out settlers in 1624, and a colony was founded on Manhattan Island called New Amsterdam. The colonists bought the land from the Native Americans with 60 guilders' (about $40) worth of miscellaneous goods.

Context

These words were inscribed on the pedestal of the Statue of Liberty in 1903, in which the New World addresses the Old:

Give me your tired, your poor,

Your huddled masses yearning to breathe free

The wretched refuse of your teeming shore.

Send these, the homeless, tempest-tossed to me,

I lift my lamp beside the golden door!

(Emma Lazarus 1849–87)

wanted to create a land of opportunity where success did not depend on birth or privilege but on hard work and courage.

America has often portrayed itself as a melting pot, a nation to which people of completely different backgrounds can come and be welcomed. It presents itself as a land of freedom and opportunity for all, although originally 'all' meant only northern Europeans.

Industrialisation

In the nineteenth century, another route to making a fortune was created by the Industrial Revolution. The mechanisation of American society was supposed to bring progress and increased order, but industrialisation often had the reverse effect as the safety and welfare of the workers were neglected in the pursuit of high profits. Industrialisation brought prosperity for the nation, turning the United States into a great world power, and wealth for the few.

Social context

America after the First World War

The outbreak of the war in 1914 took most Americans completely by surprise. Although they felt horror and pity at the newspaper reports, they also felt relief that they were not involved. However, in January 1917, Germany embarked on a policy of sinking all ships; so reluctantly America joined the war in April.

By September 1918, more than a million American troops were involved, and, in the Battle of Argonne, at which both Nick and Gatsby were supposedly present, they inflicted one of the great defeats on the Germans which helped to bring an end to the war. Many Americans were injured or killed, and those who survived thought of it as having been a pointless and destructive slaughter in which they had been forced to participate as a result of the ineptness of their parents' generation.

The Roaring Twenties

The cessation of hostilities meant that munitions, uniforms, food and other provisions for the army were no longer in demand. Inflation continued to be extremely high and loans to the Allies ceased in

1920, which meant that Europeans could no longer buy American exports. President Harding's administration was plagued by scandal and corruption, as well as opposition mounted both by unions and by organised crime, the leaders of which wielded immense power. In the efforts of management to rebuild the wealth of the country after the war, Harding supported it in labour disputes. Both Harding and his successor, Calvin Coolidge, brought in tax legislation that benefited the wealthy, widening the gap between rich and poor, as Fitzgerald demonstrates.

Nevertheless, for the country, the 1920s were a period of uninterrupted economic progress. This was the decade that changed the image of America from a log cabin to a thrusting skyscraper. The first examples of these new high-rise buildings with steel frames and elevators were built in Chicago at the end of the nineteenth century, but New York was soon competing with them for the highest building. New York City's role as an ever-growing world trade centre together with the rising prices of building plots encouraged many ambitious companies to commission skyscrapers.

Prohibition

Depression in agriculture led to migration from farms to cities, changing the face of America as people moved to urban areas where the new prosperity was to be found. However, rural America, the home of white Protestants who still held to Benjamin Franklin's virtues of thrift, hard work and self-denial, achieved a dramatic victory that was to help shape the next decade: in January 1920, the Eighteenth Amendment to the Constitution outlawed the manufacture, sale and transportation of intoxicating liquor. The main force for Prohibition came from Protestants who believed it would improve society. Predictably, perhaps, the demand for alcohol was actually increased by Prohibition, and ruthless bootleggers like Al Capone made millions of dollars through illegal alcohol sales, becoming wealthy and powerful men. Gangsterism provided a means of rapid upward mobility for men like Gatsby but, as with the drug scene today, many violent crimes were directly linked to violations of Prohibition, and Fitzgerald hints at these as he weaves a web of mystery around Gatsby.

Liberation

The veterans of the First World War wanted to forget their experiences in a hurry. Young people turned their backs on politics and the struggle of the daily grind and were determined to have a good time while they could. They rebelled against old-fashioned ways of thinking, and women, too, having entered the workforce when the men went to war,

Context

The Plaza Hotel, with 19 storeys, was built in 1907. At 60 storeys, the tallest building in Fitzgerald's New York was the Woolworth Building, completed in 1913.

Context

Bootleggers (people who make, transport and/or sell illegal alcohol) flourished during Prohibition. The term originated because they concealed flasks of alcohol in the leggings of boots.

were unwilling to give up the social and economic freedom they had gained. In addition, the Nineteenth Amendment of 1920 gave women the right to vote. In a symbolic show of emancipation, women cut their hair short, abandoned their corsets, and reinvented themselves as 'flappers'.

Flappers

The flapper became the representative symbol of the age. Young women bobbed their hair, favoured straight short dresses, wore make-up, smoked, drank alcohol, drove sports cars and generally flouted conventional social and sexual mores. The new urban-based mass media were becoming increasingly widespread and members of the postwar generation looked to the East in their search for prosperity and excitement. Like Fitzgerald's characters, they saw New York as the place to be. Here the movie industry was rapidly developing, Tin Pan Alley set the tone for what Fitzgerald dubbed the Jazz Age and life was fun.

Although the fun was directly experienced by only a privileged minority, the mass production of radios and the proliferation of magazines and newspapers meant that ordinary people could enjoy this life from the sidelines.

The economy

Boom

The total of national wealth rose from about $187 million in 1912 to $450 million in 1929. This economic boom was fuelled by new industries, bringing inventions such as automobiles, refrigerators, telephones, radios, vacuum cleaners and food processors to many American homes. Iron, steel, glass, rubber and roads were needed, so these industries also boomed. The new products had to be advertised to convince people that they could not do without all these material possessions, so the advertising industry blossomed. Advertisements were not only placed in newspapers and magazines but also on huge billboards beside highways and railways to attract the attention of passers-by.

Most people could not afford to buy the goods outright, leading to a tremendous growth in financial services, providing credit for hire purchase. Even ordinary people could have everything, although it meant that they would struggle to make the repayments. The vast majority of people were trapped in debt and could only dream that one day they would make the breakthrough, symbolised for Wilson by the opportunity to make money on Tom's car.

As mass production revolutionised the automobile industry, the car became a potent symbol of the age. It provided mobility to almost everyone, and it gave a new social freedom to young women. However, the car brought problems as well as benefits. In 1925, cars were responsible for the deaths of 25,000 people, 17,500 of them pedestrians.

Bust

Between 1922 and 1929, dividends from stock rose by 108%, corporate profits increased by 76% and wages rose by 33%. However, even in the prosperous days of Calvin Coolidge's presidency, there were more than 600 bank failures every year. Businesses put their profits into investments, and employees were encouraged to spend their savings on buying up stock in their companies, and even to buy 'on the margin', with money they did not have, intending to pay their creditor out of the profits when the shares were sold. There were no effective means for ensuring that bankers or stockbrokers were honest and many were not. The financiers of New York were the same people who had formerly looked for bonanzas as the West was opened up and its resources exploited, and they brought the same capacity for selfish exploitation to the bond market, which Nick Carraway is eager to enter.

Eventually, the bubble burst and the Wall Street Crash of 1929 brought an end to the Roaring Twenties. Fitzgerald was writing *The Great Gatsby* five years before the stock market crash and, although he could not have foreseen this particular event, there is a strong suggestion that, unless the hedonistic lifestyle of people like Tom and Daisy was curbed, it would lead to disaster: 'they smashed up things and creatures and then retreated back into their money or their vast carelessness…and let other people clean up the mess they had made' (p. 170).

Racism

As well as reflecting the economic situation in his novel, Fitzgerald reflects the contemporary fear of immigrants who were not white Anglo-Saxon Protestants. After the war, immigration soon returned to pre-war levels and both unions and business leaders lobbied against immigrants, who, they believed, were taking jobs away from American citizens. In response, Congress passed a series of bills and laws setting immigrant quotas and discriminating against people from southern and eastern Europe and from Asia.

Fitzgerald's use of a first person narrator means that the racist attitudes of his characters are not necessarily his, but, to a modern reader at least,

> **Context**
>
> In 1895 only four trucks and passenger cars had been made. By 1919, production figures had risen to 7,565,446.

❮ Top ten *quotation*

> **Context**
>
> After the war, appalling race riots broke out in the North, where former slaves from the South had gone to fill the war-built factories, and in the South a new Ku Klux Klan began to arise, viciously attacking Jews and Catholics as well as African Americans.

they provide an ironic reflection on the American Dream and the words inscribed on the Statue of Liberty.

Cultural context

New York

Fitzgerald makes a number of allusions to people, places and events that set his novel firmly in New York City. He puts New York at the centre of American business, wealth, the entertainment industry, crime and social exclusiveness, using detail that locates the novel precisely in the early 1920s. However, he does not take a documentary approach. Even the geography of the area is changed to fit his purposes and the allusions are made with a lightness of touch that suggests an artist using collage to create an impressionistic backdrop to a story of urban America.

Geography

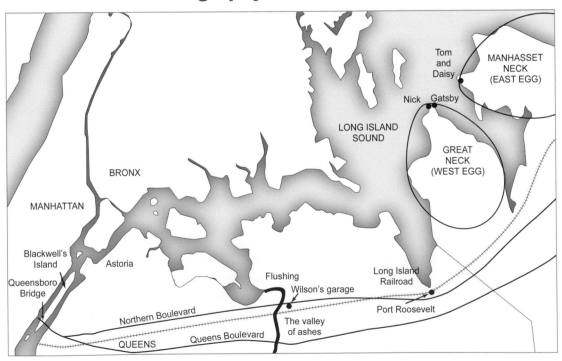

Long Island: 'East Egg' to Manhattan

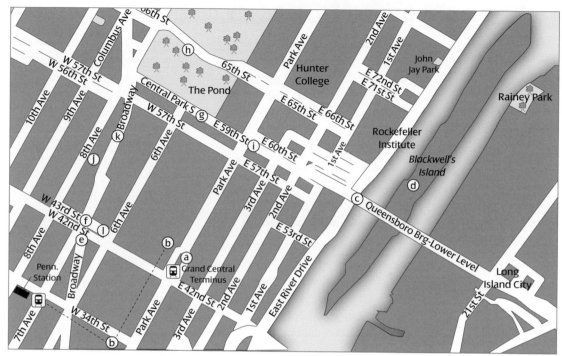

The streets of central New York

New York City is located on the north-eastern coast of the United States. The boroughs of Queens and Brooklyn are on the western end of Long Island, so, when Fitzgerald locates his characters in East and West Eggs, they are just outside the city boundary. He has made up new names for Great Neck, where the Fitzgeralds lived from 1922 to 1924, and Manhasset Neck, and has also changed the shape, creating 'a pair of enormous eggs'. The tip of Manhasset was an enclave of the fashionable, respectable wealthy, whose fortunes had been made in the nineteenth century, whereas Great Neck was home to those who had acquired their fortunes more recently and more adventurously.

When they travel to the city, Fitzgerald's characters have to cross a 'small foul river' (p. 26) in the valley of ashes.

When Gatsby drives to the city, he passes the fictional Port Roosevelt and takes Nick on a detour through Astoria, presumably to show off his car.

Context

Flushing Creek used to meander through salt marshes, but in the nineteenth century, the land around Flushing Creek was acquired by the Brooklyn Ash Removal Company, which turned the marshes into a landfill site for garbage, horse manure and ashes from coal-burning furnaces.

The entertainment industry

There are various references to people in the entertainment industry as Nick describes Gatsby's parties. Among the real people mentioned are Joe Frisco, a vaudeville performer, and Gilda Gray, a popular dancer who appeared in the Ziegfeld Follies on Broadway. The owl-eyed man compares Gatsby with David Belasco, a playwright, impresario, director and theatrical producer famous for bringing a new standard of naturalism to the American stage, and thus Fitzgerald confirms that Gatsby's house is a set to support the part he is playing.

Organised crime

It was difficult to enforce Prohibition because, as Fitzgerald shows, people could acquire as much alcohol as they wanted. In rural areas, people made their own hooch (or moonshine) with illegal stills, but in towns people relied on bootleggers to satisfy their demands. Those with money could easily get hold of whatever they wanted and had no compunction about doing so, which effectively blurred the lines of demarcation between what was legal and illegal, moral and immoral.

By 1925, there were about 100,000 illegal drinking dens, or speakeasies, in New York City alone, and Fitzgerald indicates that much of Gatsby's fortune comes from selling alcohol illegally.

Arnold Rothstein

Fitzgerald's real-life source for Meyer Wolfshiem was Arnold Rothstein, a businessman and gangster who became a famous kingpin of organised crime and was widely reputed to have been behind baseball's Black Sox Scandal in which the 1919 World Series was fixed.

Fitzgerald emphasises Wolfshiem's Jewish race, suggesting that, since the establishment was the preserve of north Europeans, for other cultural groups, gambling and crime seemed to be the only way to build up a fortune.

Wolfshiem reminisces about the old Metropole, the saloon outside which 'Rosy' Rosenthal had been gunned down. (See Chapter IV commentary.)

Literary context

Romanticism

The Romantic period refers to a movement in the arts and ways of thinking that pervaded Europe at the end of the eighteenth century and the beginning of the nineteenth. Many writers, artists and musicians reacted against the neo-Classical Age of Reason that characterised eighteenth-century thought. Instead of prizing reason and logical thinking, the new thinkers insisted that the emotional side of human responses was more important, that the brain should learn from the heart and from natural instinct, and that the imagination held purer truths than the mind. Fitzgerald's favourite poet was John Keats. In *The Great Gatsby*, Fitzgerald emulates Keats's ability to write about a memory with all the freshness and spontaneity of the moment he experienced it.

Taking it ▶
Further

Listen to Fitzgerald reading 'Ode to a Nightingale' and watch a brief film clip of Fitzgerald on www.sc.edu/fitzgerald/voice.html

Early American writers

The original Romantics rejected urban life for nature, but the rural landscape in Europe was very different from the dramatic wild landscapes of America with their extreme climate, their wolves and bears, and the Native Americans who were fighting desperately to protect their lands. A new genre of novels emerged based on the life of the cowboys and the pioneers in 'The Wild West'. Novels like *Hopalong Cassidy*, written by Clarence E. Mulford (published in 1904) fed people's dreams with stories of legendary possibilities for new opportunities and individual freedoms. It is in a copy of this novel that James Gatz wrote his schedule (p. 164).

Benjamin Franklin set out just such a schedule to illustrate how he organised his life. He had written under a pseudonym in *Poor Richard's Almanac*. This was an annual publication containing a miscellany of bits and pieces, including memorable sayings such as: 'Early to bed and early to rise, makes a man healthy, wealthy and wise.' These aphorisms optimistically sold dreams of wealth made very easily, just by leading a simple lifestyle. A popular nineteenth-century novelist who fostered this vision of golden opportunities was the Reverend Horatio Alger, who wrote stories in which, through hard work, determination, courage, and concern for others, his characters achieved enough wealth and success to have a solid stake in society.

Context

Benjamin Franklin (1706–90) was one of the Founding Fathers of America. A newspaper editor, writer, scientist and politician, he was influential in forming American values and character, combining Enlightenment tolerance with the Puritan values of hard work, education and opposition to authoritarianism.

Alger encouraged all men to believe that the American Dream was within their reach but, like young Gatz, many did not follow his advice on how to achieve it, regarding wealth as essential for the pursuit of happiness; the Declaration of Independence had stated that this was an 'unalienable right'. This fostered among Americans a belief that they could achieve anything if they worked hard enough. Fitzgerald challenges the moral naivety of Alger's books in *The Great Gatsby*, because none of his characters has achieved success solely through hard work. Even Nick Carraway's grandfather's brother made his fortune because he paid for a substitute to go to the Civil War for him.

...none of his characters has achieved success solely through hard work

Realism

However, towards the end of the nineteenth century, there were writers who aimed to portray American life as it actually was and not as they would have liked it to be. Samuel Langhorne Clemens, writing as Mark Twain, rejected Romanticism to write about people and society as he saw them. In *Huckleberry Finn*, he faithfully reproduced the colloquial speech of an uneducated boy, living outside society. The story focuses on the young boy's belief in the right thing to do, even though the society of the time, before slavery was abolished, believed it was wrong. In offering an unbiased, accurate representation of society, and confronting the problems of the individual, Realists exposed the hypocrisy of 'civilised' society.

Fitzgerald adds realistic touches to his Romantic descriptions that neatly puncture the hypocrisy of society. Gatsby's house, a factual imitation of some Hôtel de Ville in Normandy built a decade earlier by a wealthy brewer who wanted to recreate the Middle Ages, had been sold by his children with the black wreath still on the door. Clearly the 'period' craze had quickly passed and his children wasted no time grieving before getting their hands on his money (pp. 85–86). Even Nick's romantic evocation of the arrival of the Dutch sailors is tinged with realism as he describes how the trees 'pandered' to them (p. 171). The verb 'pander' has derogatory connotations from Shakespeare's Pandarus, who is presented as a cynical pimp. Fitzgerald's implication here is that the freshness of the New World, symbolised by the trees, encouraged the sailors to plunder the land. He suggests a corruption at the heart of the American Dream that occurred when European settlers made nature into a commodity.

...European settlers made nature into a commodity

Naturalism

The Realists' rejection of Romanticism and of the belief that man could shape his own future laid the foundation for Naturalism, a movement whose authors portrayed their characters as victims of social forces over which they had little or no control. Naturalists explored their characters, usually working class, through their relationships to their surroundings, usually urban. One of the most influential writers of this movement was Upton Sinclair, who exposed corruption in the Chicago meat-packing industry by focusing on the appalling living and working conditions of the poor, the exploitation of women and children in the factories and the hopelessness prevalent among the workers. Fitzgerald's portrayal of the valley of ashes and the despair of the ash-grey men who inhabit it provides a stark contrast with the lives of the wealthy and exposes their lack of social conscience. Even Nick, who seems to empathise with their hopelessness, hypocritically fails to tell the truth at the inquest and so leaves Wilson branded as a madman.

Modernism

Although Romanticism in literature was regarded as old-fashioned in the 1920s, Fitzgerald revived it by blending its imagery with the modern world. Throughout the novel, Fitzgerald uses words we associate with Romanticism, such as 'bloomed', 'singing breeze', and 'enchanted', and juxtaposes them with technological words and images. At the Buchanans' mansion, 'the crimson room bloomed with light' (p. 22), but Daisy had extinguished the candles and the light was electric. 'Like silver idols', Daisy and Jordan lay on an enormous couch, weighing down their dresses against 'the singing breeze', but this is not a Romantic natural breeze — it sings because of the electricity powering the fans (p. 110). The green light that represents Gatsby's hopes and dreams is described as 'enchanted' (p. 90), but it is an electric light, installed to guide boats on Long Island Sound.

Fitzgerald was one of the key postwar writers to employ Realistic and Naturalistic techniques to spearhead a Modernist movement. Modernism was an international movement that advocated innovation in all the arts. In America especially, a literature was needed that would explain what had happened and what was happening to society. Modernist writers were concerned to reveal the way people think. It is the internal, rather than the external, world that is important, and Fitzgerald uses complex patterns of symbols, myths and journeys to explore this. In *The*

Fitzgerald uses words we associate with Romanticism… juxtaposed with technological words and images

Great Gatsby, what really counts is not the novel's plot, but the effect of events on Nick, the narrator. To explore Nick's thoughts and feelings fully, the others remain shadowy because we are given no insight into their thoughts and feelings. Without this, we either rely on Nick's interpretation, or we draw assumptions from his observations of their expressions or behaviour.

For Modernists the specific was more important than the general so, in *The Great Gatsby*, we always know exactly where we are geographically and chronologically. Fitzgerald evokes specific pieces of music and describes detailed fashions. His minor characters are linked by specific references to the worlds of organised crime, entertainment, business or finance. Yet the novel is by no means a documentary. Fitzgerald uses real details as artists working on a collage might use cuttings from magazines and newspapers to evoke a specific era as they explore their themes.

By employing a narrator who is a relatively minor participant in the story but from whose point of view the reader learns about events, Fitzgerald, like Henry James and Joseph Conrad, gives his readers a series of scenes with the most significant parts either left to the imagination or reported through a third party. Joseph Conrad developed this narrative technique in *Lord Jim* (1900) and in *Heart of Darkness* (1902) and, like Conrad, Fitzgerald holds back key events and reveals them in a different order to enhance the mystery around Gatsby and to produce an intricately complex narrative structure.

Symbolism

Modernist writers were influenced by Freud's theory of an image-language of dreams (see p. 81). They attacked society's problems by using symbolism to make their own judgements on modern life. Fitzgerald's symbol of the eyes of Dr T. J. Eckleburg is a powerful indictment of contemporary American life. Another powerful image is Dan Cody's yacht, which, Nick tells us, represented for the young James Gatz 'all the beauty and glamour in the world' (p. 96). Thus Fitzgerald links Gatz's romantic dreams with the sordid materialism of Cody's past.

The First World War had a deep impact on American thought and development. Like other postwar works, *The Great Gatsby* conveys a mood of disillusionment with society and despair at its loss of values. It is a story of a careless, aimless, materialistic society of vast wealth that tramples over the sterile world of the poor. T. S. Eliot's poem *The Waste Land* (1922) offers similarly bleak images of sterility, death and despair in the postwar world, and Fitzgerald actually uses the title of Eliot's poem in his description of the valley of ashes. Fitzgerald echoes the emptiness of the woman's life in Eliot's poem who asks: 'What shall we do tomorrow? What shall we ever do?' when Daisy asks 'What'll we do with ourselves this afternoon?...and the day after that, and the next thirty years?' (p. 113).

A work of art

Before beginning *The Great Gatsby*, Fitzgerald reread Conrad's preface to *The Nigger of the Narcissus* (1897), and this had a significant influence on his writing of the novel. Conrad felt very strongly that the novel was an art form, and 'A work that aspires, however humbly, to the condition of art should carry its justification in every line'. Conrad felt that, while a novelist should be influenced by different literary 'formulas', they should 'abandon him — even on the very threshold of the temple — to the stammerings of his conscience and to the outspoken consciousness of the difficulties of his work.' Fitzgerald followed this advice closely and this is the main reason why early critics judged his third novel such an improvement on his previous ones.

> **Taking it Further** ▶
>
> Read Conrad's Preface to *The Nigger of the Narcissus* and assess its impact on Fitzgerald: www.online-literature.com/conrad/the-narcissus/0/.

Critical context

Contemporary criticism

When *The Great Gatsby* was first published in 1925, many reviewers recognised it as a fulfilment of the promise Fitzgerald had shown in his previous novels. Isabel Paterson wrote that he 'managed somehow to pour his glowing youth on the page before it could escape forever'. Others, such as H. L. Mencken, a critic for whom Fitzgerald had the greatest respect, were more overtly critical. He called the novel a 'glorified anecdote', complaining that it is 'simply a story', and that 'only Gatsby himself genuinely lives and breathes'. He dismissed the other characters as 'mere marionettes'. Nevertheless, he was full of praise for Fitzgerald's craftsmanship and the 'charm and beauty of the writing'.

The novel excited considerable interest among other writers. Gertrude Stein told Fitzgerald that, in *The Great Gatsby*, he was 'creating the contemporary world' in the same way that W. M. Thackeray had in his novels. This is a significant choice of verb, implying that he was not merely reflecting 1920s America but helping to construct it. T. S. Eliot was

also 'interested and excited' by it, grandly claiming that it represented 'the first step that American fiction has taken since Henry James'.

Posthumous revival and criticism

In spite of its largely favourable reception by the critics, the novel did not sell well. However, Fitzgerald's death in 1940 reawakened interest in the writer and his books. Several obituaries praised *The Great Gatsby*, but some felt that it was a product of its time and was already outdated. Fitzgerald's writing was linked to his life, and his decline into alcoholism was seen by some as being related to what they felt was his inability to fulfil his early promise.

William Troy

Nevertheless, several new editions appeared in the 1940s and William Troy claimed that *The Great Gatsby* was a characteristically American novel. He argued that Fitzgerald manages to achieve something like T. S. Eliot's 'objective correlative' (an external equivalent for an internal state of mind) by splitting his own divided self between the two central characters. He is able to observe objectively through 'the ordinary but quite sensible narrator', as well as to bring to life, in Jay Gatsby, Fitzgerald's own Romantic dreams. Troy claimed that Gatsby is a 'mythological creation', a product of the wish-fulfilment of a whole nation: 'Gatsby becomes…a symbol of America itself, dedicated to "the service of a vast, vulgar and meretricious beauty".'

> Fitzgerald…splits his own divided self between the two central characters

He observed that the novelist had employed the technical device of an involved and sympathetic narrator, in the tradition of Henry James and Joseph Conrad, which makes for 'some of the most priceless values in fiction — economy, suspense, intensity. And these values *The Great Gatsby* possesses to a rare degree.' By linking Fitzgerald with established writers such as Eliot, James and Conrad, Troy was signalling that *The Great Gatsby* was worthy of academic study.

Arthur Mizener

Another 1940s critic who rated the novel highly and suggested ways in which its themes and techniques could be more deeply explored and analysed was Arthur Mizener. Like Troy, he explored the novel's 'modified first-person form' and Nick's importance as narrator. He called the novel a kind of 'tragic pastoral', with the East representing urban sophistication as well as corruption, and the West representing simple virtue. Mizener explored the title of the novel, observing that: 'Insofar as Gatsby represents the simple virtue which Fitzgerald associates with the West, he is really a great man; insofar as he achieves the kind of notoriety which the East accords success of his kind, he is about as great as Barnum was.' He judged that the irony of the book lay in Gatsby's inability to understand himself and how society judged him. Mizener recognised that Fitzgerald was fundamentally a poet, and he praised the 'formal perfection' of *The Great Gatsby*.

The new criticism of the 1950s

In the 1950s, Fitzgerald began to be studied in many American universities and *The Great Gatsby* achieved the status of a classic American novel. Lionel Trilling was the first of many to make the claim that Gatsby represents America: 'Gatsby, divided between power and dream, comes inevitably to stand for America itself. Ours is the only nation that prides itself upon a dream and gives its name to one, "the American Dream".'

The academic debates had begun. In 1955, R. W. Stallman wrote an essay in which he argued that it had become a great novel because Gatsby is 'a modern Icarus…who…belongs not exclusively to one epoch of American civilisation but rather to all history inasmuch as all history repeats in cycle form what Gatsby represents — America itself'. Troy had argued that Nick was an admirable character who had grown in moral perception by the end of the novel. Stallman disagreed, calling him 'a prig with holier-than-thou airs'. Mizener had interpreted the novel as a 'tragic pastoral', celebrating an idealised version of rural life in the Midwest; whereas Stallman argued that Fitzgerald showed that the apparent division between the corrupt urban East and the moral rural Midwest exists only in Nick's imagination. Since these essays many critics have joined in the debates and written books analysing *The Great Gatsby*.

Ethnic criticism

Not until 1947 was Fitzgerald first criticised for the anti-Semitism of his presentation of Meyer Wolfshiem. Not until 1967 was he criticised for his derogatory portrayals of African-Americans, as well as the way Nick interprets the American Dream as being only for people like himself. In 1973, Peter Gregg Slater observed that Native Americans were ignored in Nick's vision of the founding moment of America. It is easy to criticise the novel for its narrow outlook, but it is important to remember that it reflected the attitudes of the 1920s. We should be wary of judging Fitzgerald for being a product of his time.

Context

Icarus is a character in Greek mythology who attempted to escape from exile using wings his father had made. He flew too close to the sun, the wax in his wings melted and he fell into the sea. He is a common literary symbol of heroic audacity.

Context

In the USA in the first half of the twentieth century, Jews were discriminated against in employment, universities, membership of organisations and access to residential areas. Jews were one of the targets of the Ku Klux Klan.

Feminist criticism

Feminist critics attempt to describe and interpret women's experience as depicted in literature. They question the long-standing dominant male ideologies, patriarchal attitudes and male interpretations in literature. They challenge traditional and accepted male ideas about the nature of women and how women are, according to male writers, supposed to feel, act and think. Fitzgerald limits his portrayal of his women characters by having as his narrator a misogynist who declares that 'Dishonesty in a woman is a thing you never blame deeply' (pp. 58–59). Such a narrator cannot be expected to reveal any empathy with a woman's feelings.

In 1977, Judith Fetterley published *The Resisting Reader: A Feminist Approach to American Fiction*, in which she argues that, with very few exceptions, at the time she was writing, American literature had been mostly written by men and so their attempts to define what it means to be American were made from a male perspective. She argues that, in *The Great Gatsby*, Fitzgerald portrays America as female, writing of her green breast that 'had once pandered in whispers to the last and greatest of all human dreams' (p. 171), whereas the dreamers are male. 'Daisy's failure of Gatsby is symbolic of the failure of America to live up to the expectations in the imagination of the men who "discovered" it. America is female; to be American is male; and the quintessential American experience is betrayal by a woman.'

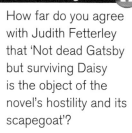

*Pause for **Thought***

How far do you agree with Judith Fetterley that 'Not dead Gatsby but surviving Daisy is the object of the novel's hostility and its scapegoat'?

Feminist critics take Nick to task for his double standards: he excuses Gatsby's lies because he is reconstructing himself to achieve his dream. Gatsby's whole life is a pose but, as soon as Nick realises why, he enthuses that 'he came alive to me, delivered suddenly from the womb of his purposeless splendour' (p. 76). Nick takes this image of rebirth further when he glorifies Gatsby as having sprung from 'his Platonic conception of himself. He was a son of God…and he must be about His Father's business, the service of a vast, vulgar, and meretricious beauty' (p. 95). Even while he recognises the falseness of Gatsby's dream, he speaks of it as if it were holy. By contrast, Nick accuses Daisy and Jordan of adopting poses that are inexcusable because they are designed to put men, and specifically Nick, at a disadvantage, 'as though the whole evening had been a trick of some sort to exact a contributory emotion from me' (p. 22). For Nick, women's attraction lies in their inaccessibility, and he assumes that, once Gatsby has met Daisy again, 'his count of enchanted objects had diminished by one' (p. 90). Judith Fetterley wrote: 'Nick's dishonesty goes unrecognised by most of the novel's readers: it is not perceived as dishonest because it is common, pervasive, and 'natural' to a sexist society. *The Great Gatsby* is a dishonest book because the culture from which it derives and which it reflects is radically dishonest'.

Judith Fetterley also claims that *The Great Gatsby* is a classic male drama of poor boy achieving wealth and challenging rich boy, and that the story is a struggle for power, with the prize being the girl. When the poor boy dies, it is not the rich boy who becomes the scapegoat, but Daisy, because she failed him. Nick shakes hands with Tom, but there is no such reconciliation with Daisy — she alone bears the blame.

Psychoanalytic criticism

Fitzgerald was born four years before Sigmund Freud published one of the founding texts of psychoanalysis, *The Interpretation of Dreams*, in 1900. Psychoanalytic critics see literature as like dreams. Both are fictions, inventions of the mind that, although based on reality, are not literally true. The theory is that much of what lies in the unconscious mind has been repressed, or censored, by consciousness and emerges only in disguised forms, such as dreams, or in an art form, such as painting or writing. They interpret the author's purpose in writing as being to gratify secretly some forbidden wish that has been repressed.

Fitzgerald was writing *The Great Gatsby* at the time when psychoanalytic ideas and techniques were being developed and circulated. Freud first discussed his structural model of the psyche in his 1920 essay 'Beyond the Pleasure Principle', introducing his concepts of the 'id', the 'ego' and the 'super-ego'. These concepts were formalised and elaborated upon three years later in *The Ego and the Id*. According to Freud's theory, the id represents our inner desires, amoral and egocentric, ruled by the pleasure/pain principle. The super-ego is a symbolic internalisation of our upbringing and cultural regulations that acts as our conscience. The ego's task is to find a balance between these two opposing forces so that we can function in the real world.

Fitzgerald followed his inner desires and followed (or rather led) the decadent lifestyle of his generation, but his tragedy was that his super-ego made him despise himself for doing so. Like Fitzgerald himself, Nick Carraway shows evidence of being torn between his id and his super-ego, 'simultaneously enchanted and repelled by the inexhaustible variety of life' (p. 37). Nick has a highly developed super-ego, therefore his upbringing and training in the rules of society lead him to disapprove of all the other characters in the novel. However, his id, representing his inner desires, encourages him to forgive Gatsby, excusing his dishonesty because he admires, perhaps envies, Gatsby's romantic vision. Thus he is able to present Gatsby as 'Great', a tragic

> **Context**
>
> Sigmund Freud (1856–1939), was a Jewish-Austrian psychiatrist, who founded psychoanalysis. His originality made him one of the most influential thinkers of the early 20th century.

Nick…torn between his id and his super-ego

❮ Top ten *quotation*

hero. At the beginning he tells his readers that Gatsby 'represented everything for which I have an unaffected scorn', but 'there was something gorgeous about him, some heightened sensitivity to the promises of life' (p. 8). Fitzgerald uses a driving metaphor to illustrate how Nick's highly developed super-ego is preventing him from indulging his id, and from forming meaningful relationships: 'I am slow-thinking and full of interior rules that act as brakes on my desires' (p. 59).

Nick's imagination and his dreams offer the key to understanding his character and how the events in the novel change him. We learn that his ego tries to balance his desires and his conscience through a dream of secret casual affairs with romantic women he meets on Fifth Avenue, to whom he does not have to commit himself (p. 57). By the time he returns to the Midwest, Nick's 'fantastic dreams' are of West Egg, as if in a painting by El Greco (p. 167). No longer does he find the metropolitan twilight 'enchanting'. Even the moon has lost its lustre and romance, and the sky appears 'sullen', an example of the pathetic fallacy that neatly sums up his disappointed romantic dreams.

Marxist criticism

Context

Karl Marx (1818–83) was a German philosopher and political theorist. With Friedrich Engels, he was the author of *The Communist Manifesto* (1848), which interpreted society in terms of class struggle.

The Marxist perspective is that works of literature are conditioned by the economic and political forces of their social context. Not only does Fitzgerald explore class tensions between the wealthy and the despairing poor who scrape a living among the ash-heaps of New York's waste, but his narrator explores the divisions between East Egg and West Egg. Those who live in East Egg glory in inherited wealth and think themselves superior to those, like Fitzgerald himself, who are self-made men having become rich in entertainment, the financial sector or crime.

Fitzgerald writes about New York, giving valuable insights into the negative aspects of the postwar economic boom. His novel can be read as a penetrating criticism of the uncaring, materialistic and corrupt ruling classes. Nick's criticism of Tom and Daisy (p. 170) can be read as a prophecy of the Wall Street Crash and the Great Depression. Central to the story is the allegation that, at the inquest, the authorities put the blame for Gatsby's murder on Mr Wilson, 'in order that the case might remain in its simplest form'; to investigate the truth might have uncovered corruption at a high level.

Working with the text

Meeting the Assessment Objectives

AO1: Articulate creative, informed and relevant responses to literary texts, using appropriate terminology and concepts, and coherent, accurate written expression.

For AO1, you need to write fluently, structuring your essay carefully, guiding your reader clearly through your line of argument and using the sophisticated vocabulary, including critical terminology, which is appropriate to an A-level essay. You will need to use frequent embedded quotations to give evidence of close detailed knowledge, and you should demonstrate familiarity with the whole text.

AO2: Demonstrate detailed critical understanding in analysing the ways in which structure, form and language shape meaning in literary texts.

For AO2, it is a good idea to practise writing in analytical sentences, comprising a brief quotation or close reference, a definition or description of the feature you intend to analyse, an explanation of how Fitzgerald has used this feature, and an evaluation of why he chose to use it.

...practise writing in analytical sentences

AO3i: Explore connections and comparisons between different literary texts.

Your examination board may require you to compare and contrast one or more other texts with *The Great Gatsby,* and you should try to find specific points of comparison, rather than merely generalising. If this AO is assessed in single-text questions, you could explore the connections with another postwar work such as T. S. Eliot's *The Waste Land.* Other useful additional texts would be Fitzgerald's own short stories; 'Absolution', which was originally part of *The Great Gatsby,* deals with

Taking it Further ▶

Read 'Absolution' on http://
gutenberg.net.au/fsf/
ABSOLUTION.html and
'Winter Dreams' on
www.sc.edu/fitzgerald/
winterd/winter.html.

the early life of a boy like James Gatz. 'Winter Dreams' deals with a poor boy, Dexter Green, attracted to the life of the rich; although here Fitzgerald uses an omniscient narrator rather than a partially involved narrator. Both Gatsby and Dexter dream of the shallow superficial glitter of a society which pursues wealth. Like Gatsby, for whom Daisy's popularity 'increased her value', Dexter is attracted to Irene because she was 'sturdily popular, so intensely great'. There is a significant contrast at the end when the omniscient narrator of 'Winter Dreams' states 'The dream was gone', whereas Nick can only speculate that Gatsby 'must have felt that he had lost the old warm world, paid a high price for living too long with a single dream'.

Alternatively you could choose to trace a common theme which appears in *The Great Gatsby* and one or more other texts such as love, the American Dream, the role of women or appearance and reality.

AO3ii: Look at various possible different interpretations and use these to develop your own.

This implies looking at various critical views as well as thinking about what you and your fellow students think. Because Nick is an unreliable narrator, there are plenty of opportunities for you to explore different interpretations of events. For example, you may think that his presentation of Daisy and Jordan is unsympathetic and judgemental and offer another possible reading of the detailed observations he makes.

Nick accepts the inquest's findings that Wilson murdered Gatsby. However there is evidence which suggests that Fitzgerald intended to raise the possibility that this might have been a contract killing, carried out by a hit man hired by one of Gatsby's business associates. When Gatsby starts his affair with Daisy, he dismisses all his servants and replaces them with 'some people Wolfshiem wanted to do something for' (p. 109). Fitzgerald makes a point of saying that the chauffeur, 'one of Wolfshiem's protégés', heard the shots but did nothing. Nick firmly believes that the servants knew that Gatsby was dead before he arrived. This suggests that Wolfshiem planted his servants in Gatsby's house to keep an eye on Gatsby. It is possible that Gatsby was double-crossing Wolfshiem. After all, Gatsby offers Nick 'a little business on the side' and reassures him that he 'wouldn't have to do any business with Wolfshiem' (p. 80). Additionally, Wilson did not fight in the war, and he is too poor to own a car. It seems unlikely that he would own a gun or have the skill to kill with the first shot a man floating on an airbed without puncturing it.

You could suggest that it is ironic that Nick might have totally misread the whole story. Instead of Gatsby being the tragic hero of a romantic love story, he might have been merely another victim of internecine strife in the criminal underworld. Instead of Wilson being a romantic hero, he might have just been an innocent victim of chance. Their deaths may have had nothing to do with any of the characters whom Nick thought so crucial to his two interlinked triangles of love and betrayal. If Fitzgerald did employ an unreliable narrator in order to suggest this, then interesting issues are raised.

AO4: Demonstrate understanding of the significance and influence of the contexts in which literary texts are written and received.

Some awareness of the effect of the First World War on the American economy and the American psyche is essential here. You should also demonstrate understanding of the historical roots of the American Dream and the significance of the symbolism of East and West in America. The most significant literary influences on Fitzgerald's writing are the poet John Keats, and the Polish writer Joseph Conrad.

Men's attitudes to women were markedly different, and you also need to be aware of the different attitudes towards race prevalent in the 1920s; Nick now seems unpleasantly anti-Semitic in his comments about Wolfshiem and racist in his attitude towards his Finnish housekeeper and Black Americans. His use of the word '**holocaust**' to describe the scene of the deaths of just two men was hyperbolic at the time of writing but now sounds unacceptably disrespectful to the victims of Nazi Germany.

*Task **13***

Find evidence that Nick may be seen as racist.

Holocaust great destruction or loss of life, or the source of that destruction, especially fire

Essay writing

The following sections give guidance on writing essays. Sample essays at A grade and C grade are provided online at **www.philipallan.co.uk/ literatureguidesonline**.

Extract-based essay questions

Here are the questions to address when analysing any given extract from this novel:

- Why has Fitzgerald included this passage in the novel? What is its importance?
- How does this passage fit into the narrative structure of the novel?
- Which of the themes is Fitzgerald evoking here, and how does this passage fit into his treatment of that theme in the whole novel?
- What previous scenes do we need to recall in order to understand the implications of this passage?

- Does this extract foreshadow any future scenes?
- It is a first-person narrative, so how reliable is Nick's account at this point?
- Is there any evidence that Nick is self-consciously crafting his narrative?
- Is there any evidence of Nick's ambivalent attitudes?
- Is there any evidence that Nick's narrative is enhanced by his imagination?
- What does this passage reveal about Nick's character, feelings and his thoughts?
- Does Fitzgerald use any recurring images or symbols in this passage? If so, analyse how they fit into the overall pattern.
- If there is description, what mood is Fitzgerald evoking and how does he do it?
- Is there any speech in this passage? If so, what does it add to the effectiveness, and what does it tell us about the speaker?
- Are there any words, phrases or metaphors that would reward close analysis?

Whole-text questions

Make sure you know which Assessment Objectives are examined by your board and concentrate on those. AO1 is assessed by looking at your whole essay and judging whether your writing skills and vocabulary are appropriate for A-level, whether your essay has been carefully planned and whether you are clearly very familiar with the whole text. The other Assessment Objectives you can plan for.

Sample question

> **How far do you agree that *The Great Gatsby* is a sordid tale of deception, adultery and murder?**

Possible approach

- Since there is no disputing the fact that the novel is about deception, adultery and murder, the question expects you to concentrate on whether this makes the story sordid. Define 'sordid' and then consider the evidence in turn.
- You could gain valuable marks for AO4 by demonstrating an understanding of the novel's various contexts. Fitzgerald sets the novel against the sordid backdrop of corruption through references to the fixing of the 1919 Baseball World Series, bootlegging, and passing

Task **14**

How would you approach a question to be marked only on AO1 and AO2 asking you to compare the ways in which Fitzgerald describes the two parties on pp. 43–56 and pp. 100–05?

counterfeit or stolen bonds. He also exposes the corruption of the police through the murder of Rosenthal and the police commissioner's collusion with Gatsby.

- You can meet the requirements of AO2 by exploring Fitzgerald's narrative technique. His use of an involved narrator blurs the boundaries between deception and honesty. Nick is not a reliable narrator and his attitude is different from the reader's.

- There is an opportunity to gain marks for AO3 by offering an alternative interpretation: Gatsby's murder could be an ennobling act of love by Wilson *or* a sordid contract killing by one of Gatsby's criminal associates.

- Attitudes to adultery are also affected by Nick's distorted moral vision. Analyse his language for AO2 to show that Tom's and Myrtle's affair is described as sordid, but Daisy's and Gatsby's affair is excused by Nick's belief in the romance of Gatsby's love.

- Having shown that you understand why this question has been set, offer evidence which disagrees with its conclusion. You could analyse evidence of Fitzgerald's lyrical prose and Nick's romantic imagination.

- You can then draw your essay to a conclusion by saying that the story could be described as sordid *but* Fitzgerald lifts it out of being base and ignoble into the genre of romance with Gatsby's 'ineffable' dream and Nick's poetic descriptions.

Comparative questions

The examiners will expect you to offer a balanced essay with equal consideration given to each text, comparing and contrasting them seamlessly throughout your essay. As always, AO1 will be assessed throughout but you can plan carefully to meet the requirements of the other AOs.

Sample question

Explore the ways in which love has been presented in two of the texts you have studied.

Possible approach comparing *The Great Gatsby* with *Captain Corelli's Mandolin*

- It is especially important in a comparative essay to decide on your line of argument before you start planning your essay. You might conclude that Fitzgerald concentrates on romantic and parental love whereas Bernières explores love in all its forms.

...decide on your line of argument before you start planning your essay

- For AO2 analysis of form, you should explore the narrative techniques of the two writers. Fitzgerald uses an involved unreliable narrator who avoids commitment in love and is cynical about the parental love of Daisy and Henry Gatz. By contrast, Bernières employs different narrative techniques and explores the concept of love widely.

- AO2 analysis of language in *The Great Gatsby* will reveal the ambivalence of Nick's attitudes. He uses mercenary language to describe Gatsby's feeling for Daisy ('value', 'bought luxury') and a semantic field of plunder ('He took what he could get, ravenously and unscrupulously'), but he also uses language of romance ('blossomed', 'incarnation', 'ripe mystery').

- In *Captain Corelli's Mandolin,* Dr Iannis's definition is: 'love itself is what is left over when being in love has burned away'. You could explore the characters in both novels to assess which ones are presented as demonstrating real love.

- For AO3, you could explore the similarity between Gatsby and Corelli who both idolise the woman of their dreams. Nick refers to Daisy as Gatsby's 'grail', and Pelagia is presented as Corelli's inspiration, like Dante's 'Beatrice' or Petrarch's 'Laura'. This leads to ambiguity since we never really know whether either man felt genuine, unselfish love.

- Examiners like to see you explore ambiguity. You could explore whether Daisy and Corelli are insincere and incapable of love or whether they have a realistic understanding of love. After all, Corelli claims that he loves both Pelagia and Antonia, and Daisy admits to Gatsby: 'I did love him (Tom) once — but I loved you too.'

- For AO4, you could explore the significance and influence of war on attitudes to love, since Bernières sets his novel during the Second World War and Fitzgerald is writing about New York society shortly after the First World War.

- For AO4, you could explore attitudes to women in 1920s USA and 1940s Greek islands and how they influence the writers' exploration of love. You will also need to show how Bernières's attitudes differ from those in his novel since he was writing in 1998.

- If we take as our definition of true love Pelagia's words about her father: 'the only man I've ever loved who loved me to the end, and never bruised my heart, and never for a single moment failed me', we will conclude that Bernières created two characters with this selfless love for another (Carlo and Dr Iannis). Fitzgerald was more cynical — all his characters 'bruise hearts'. However, you might disagree with the statement in the question, because love should always be unselfish, so one single word can do for all different kinds.

…examiners like to see you explore ambiguity

Transformational writing

Sample task

> **Write Daisy's account of her first visit to Gatsby's house. You should aim to write in Daisy's voice, building upon Scott Fitzgerald's presentation of her character and capturing aspects of the writer's chosen form, structure and language.**

Extract from answer

'His beautiful house! Like a romantic film set, and I was the heroine. It was a girlhood dream come true. Oh Jordan! When he was showing me around, he opened a cupboard full of shirts and tossed them onto the bed, an amazing kaleidoscope of divine colours and patterns and fabrics. Do you know, Jordan — they were a gift of love. You remember, when I met him, he was a young officer at Camp Taylor? He always wore his army uniform. I teased him about it once, joking that anyone would think he didn't have anything else to wear. He went very quiet and blushed with embarrassment. I quickly said that I was proud to be seen out with a lieutenant of the American army. Suddenly he burst out, "After the war I'll wear a different colour every day of the year, and I'll never wear khaki again."

As those gorgeous shirts piled up on the bed, I realised that he was wearing my colours — a white suit and a gold tie, like a daisy. I just b-burst into tears. When I realized how devoted he was, it hurt me deep inside, because I'd b-betrayed him. Tom mocked him for wearing a pink suit, but it was exactly the same shade of pink as the scarf I gave him. Because he was sulking after I teased him about his uniform, I told him that he could wear my colours like the knights of old who went into battle wearing their ladies' favours. I gave him my rose-coloured scarf, and he just stared at it for the longest time before tucking it into his jacket. Giving him the scarf was somehow a token that he was the one I'd chosen. I felt like Guinevere giving her favour to Lancelot to keep him safe when he went into battle.'

Student's own commentary

For my first person narrative, I have built on Fitzgerald's references to symbols like the nightingale in association with Daisy and continued his presentation of her as a romantic by using references to the Arthurian legend. I drew on my knowledge of the text to assume that she would be talking to her friend as she gave this account, and to provide the background information that explains her unexpected reaction to the pile of shirts.

As this is a piece of spontaneous dialogue, I have used Fitzgerald's chosen speech mannerisms including stuttering (b-burst), empty adjectives (gorgeous, divine), hyperbole (the longest time) and I have elided the first person subject pronoun with the auxiliary verb (I'd). Because Daisy is talking to a friend and there are no men present, she can speak more freely, explaining herself in complex sentences, as well as using incomplete utterances, exclamations and questions to reveal emotion.

Examiner's comments

AO1 — quality of writing:

- vocabulary appropriate to an educated American lady of the twenties
- a creative and original point of view (explaining why Daisy burst into tears)
- creating and sustaining a believable register
- varied sentence structure which reflects source text
- no unnecessary narration/storytelling/plot recount

AO2 — form, structure and language:

- sense that the language used is a 'map of the character's mind'
- using Fitzgerald's text as a template — using a first person narrator who may not be reflecting others entirely without bias
- sense that the character chosen is understood and the attitudes she displays are convincing and likely, based on a close reading of the text
- use of figurative language
- use of symbolism
- specific reflections of Fitzgerald's text which show a seamless overarching understanding of text

AO3 — different interpretations:

- offers a fresh understanding of Daisy, free from Nick Carraway's prejudices

AO4 — contexts:

- references/actions/speech appropriate to the era in which the text is set
- subtle but clear reference to Gatsby's training for the First World War

Extended commentaries

In all kinds of essay, you need to show that you can analyse form, structure and language in detail. Select key passages and practise analysing them, as well as setting them in the context of the whole novel, so that you have examples ready to include in your essays.

1 The swimming pool (p. 154)

In order to appreciate the poetic quality of Fitzgerald's writing, set out a passage as poetry and then justify your selection. One choice could be the description of what Nick saw when he hurried to the pool:

The swimming pool

There was a faint, barely perceptible movement of the water

As the fresh flow from one end urged its way toward the drain at the other.

With little ripples that were hardly the shadows of waves,

The laden mattress moved irregularly down the pool.

A small gust of wind that scarcely corrugated the surface

Was enough to disturb its accidental course with its accidental burden.

The touch of a cluster of leaves revolved it slowly,

Tracing, like the leg of transit, a thin red circle in the water.

Unlike the brutally realistic description of Myrtle's body, Fitzgerald has not mentioned Gatsby's body at all. The readers are distanced from Gatsby in death as we were in life, so that nothing will destroy the illusion. There is no expression of shock or horror, and this suggests that Nick knew what they were going to find.

Reading this paragraph in isolation, there is no indication of its subject. Instead, Nick seems mesmerised by the movement of the water. As the water flows down the pool, the mattress moves irregularly down the pool towards the drain, where the vortex carries the mattress round in gradual circles. It seems to the fanciful Nick as if it were the touch of autumn leaves that provoked this circular motion. Fitzgerald employs poetic techniques such as personification (the water…urged its way),

alliteration (fresh, flow from), assonance (touch…cluster) and rhythm (n.b. the regular iambic metre of the fourth line), to show that Nick finds a tragic romance in the death of a man whose life has not been heroic. Metaphors (shadows, corrugated) give the detail, not to events, not to Gatsby's body, but to the surface of the water, showing that Nick is so mesmerised by its movement that he fails to notice what the people with him are doing. The repetition of the adjective 'accidental' turns Gatsby into a sacrificial victim because, in Nick's view, he was not the intended victim of the gunman. Fitzgerald's choice of adjective provides a neat play on words that creates ambiguity since 'accidental' can mean both unintentional and fateful.

Separating this passage encourages us to concentrate on Fitzgerald's skill as a poet, but it is important to look at it in the context of the book, as it continues patterns that Fitzgerald has woven through the whole novel. Fitzgerald has given it a cyclical movement: Nick came east in spring; the love affair blooms through the summer until the climax on the hottest day of the year; Gatsby dies on the first day of autumn, and Nick returns to the Midwest in late autumn.

Throughout the novel, Fitzgerald has blended the natural and constructed worlds in his imagery. Here, too, the ripples on the water are so slight as to be hardly the 'shadows' of waves, but when a small gust of wind comes, the surface of the water looks like 'corrugated' paper or iron. A technological image compares the revolving mattress with the leg of a precision instrument, a transit compass, drawing a circle in the leaves. The movement of the mattress is part of a recurring pattern of stillness and movement that started when a breeze blew in through the windows of Daisy's and Tom's house and 'rippled over the wine-coloured rug, making a shadow on it as wind does on the sea' (p. 13).

2 The valley of ashes (pp. 26–27)

Immediately after the scene in the Buchanans' mansion in East Egg, which gave us a glimpse into the lives of the rich, Fitzgerald describes an area through which they must pass on their way to town. The valley of ashes is the grim underside of New York, where the garbage is dumped, but it is an essential part of it. To describe it, Fitzgerald uses adjectives from the semantic field of disbelief that suggest an unnatural landscape beyond the range of human experience, such as 'grotesque', 'fantastic' and 'transcendent'. However, most of the adjectives come from a semantic field of sterility and despair: 'desolate', 'impenetrable', 'bleak', 'foul', 'dismal'.

Fitzgerald uses a simile which draws a direct comparison between a fertile farm where crops are grown and this barren valley where 'ashes grow like wheat'. The whole landscape is created out of ash, and even the men who work there look as if they are formed out of ash. The farming metaphor emphasises by contrast the infertility of the valley. Even the grey cars give out a 'ghastly' creak, as if they are giving up the ghost before coming to rest.

Everything in the valley of ashes is grey, even the people, except for the enormous billboard with the oculist's advertisement and a block of three shops in yellow brick, sitting on the edge of the waste land. One of these is Wilson's garage. Fitzgerald's choice of yellow brick surrounded by grey makes it sound 'anaemic', like Wilson himself. Wilson is 'spiritless' and his garage is metaphorically described as a 'shadow', insubstantial and lacking in life and vitality. 'Everything in the vicinity' is veiled in dust, including the only car in the building, a wrecked Ford. The garage seems to represent all those people whose lives have been destroyed by the affluent society, and who are now ignored and abandoned. Even Nick, with his romantic imagination, is unable to see in it any more than a grotesque parody of rural life elsewhere. He romantically assumes that 'sumptuous and romantic apartments were concealed overhead', but he is wrong.

3 Myrtle's death (p. 131)

As Fitzgerald's involved narrator did not see the accident, he reports what Michaelis supposedly told the inquest, quoting the newspapers' sensational monosyllabic description of the 'death car'. The facts are embellished with emotive adverbs to satisfy the morbid curiosity of the papers' readers, describing how the car wavered 'tragically', and Myrtle's life was 'violently' extinguished.

Fitzgerald describes her body in detail after the accident and insisted to his publisher that he did not want to change the wording. Ironically, she is kneeling, a posture suggesting prayer or possibly penitence. Her infidelity has led to her death and, posthumously, she is seen to repent. Three heavily stressed monosyllables with dull plosive consonants reinforce the idea of punishment as her 'thick dark blood' mingled with the 'dust', and the choice of this word reminds us of the biblical prophecy 'Dust thou art and unto dust thou shalt return.'

The details of her injuries have implications related to her sexuality: the mouth with which she kissed Tom has been ripped, and 'her left breast was swinging loose like a flap'. The breast is a symbol of both sexuality

and maternal love, so in this image Fitzgerald graphically shows that it is her sexual infidelity that has brought about her destruction, but at the same time he reminds us that she had no children. Like the valley of ashes in which she lived, she was barren.

Nick's last words in this section reveal once again his admiration for 'the tremendous vitality she had stored so long', giving her death a poignancy we might not have expected.

Top ten quotations

1

...what foul dust floated in the wake of his dreams... (p. 8

Nick casts the blame on this 'foul dust'. Gatsby's dreams are compared with a boat, forging ahead and leaving a track where the water has been disturbed. The implication seems to be that his dreams stirred up 'foul dust', which may be Nick's judgement on Daisy and Tom, but it certainly suggests the valley of ashes that represents the dark underside of the glittering world Tom and Daisy inhabit. The other meaning of 'wake', a watch beside a corpse, foreshadows the ending.

2

...life is much more successfully looked at from a single window, after all. (p. 10)

This metaphor follows the oxymoron 'that most limited of all specialists, the "well-rounded man"'. By claiming that this is an epigram, Nick acknowledges that it was intended to be a clever, witty way of suggesting that people who are described as 'well-rounded' actually know very little about a lot of things. The metaphor suggests that, to be successful, you need to concentrate on one aspect of life, looking through a single window. This is also an interesting metaphor for Fitzgerald's narrative technique that employs a single narrator who is given only 'privileged glimpses' into other people's lives.

3

I was within and without, simultaneously enchanted and repelled by the inexhaustible variety of life. (p. 37)

This quotation sums up the position of the partially involved narrator Fitzgerald has created. Although Nick is accepted by the communities he observes, he does not really belong, so he is paradoxically both 'within and without'. His ambivalent attitude to events, and particularly to Gatsby, is revealed in his admission that he is both 'enchanted and repelled'. This is particularly significant because it effectively describes Fitzgerald's own feelings about New York society in the Roaring Twenties.

> **On Sunday morning while church bells rang in the villages alongshore, the world and its mistress returned to Gatsby's house and twinkled hilariously on his lawn. (p. 60)**

4

Fitzgerald specifically tells us that Gatsby celebrates the Sabbath Day with parties, suggesting that he seeks a mystical union, but not with God; he hopes his parties will bring him closer to Daisy. The misogyny of the narrator is revealed in the assumption that the world and everybody important in it is male. The connotations of the verb 'twinkle' are of something superficially bright, flickering intermittently, but insubstantial and ephemeral, like Christmas tree lights. By saying that the world 'twinkled' Fitzgerald exposes the emptiness of the lives of people for whom faith has been replaced by superficial hilarity.

> **...the rock of the world was founded securely on a fairy's wing... (p. 96)**

5

Fitzgerald gives a concrete image to demonstrate the impossibility of Gatsby's dreams ever coming true. As a teenager, Gatsby imagined 'the most grotesque and fantastic conceits'. Gatsby, however, persuaded himself that he could build a secure future upon them, a dream as hopeless as balancing a rock on something as insubstantial and unreal as a fairy's wing.

> **...he had committed himself to the following of a grail. (p. 142)**

6

With this metaphor, Nick romantically links Daisy and Gatsby to the Arthurian legend. The Holy Grail was the legendary cup in which Joseph of Arimathea caught the blood of Christ on the cross. In Arthurian legend, only the purest knights were permitted to undertake the sacred quest to find the grail.

> **They were careless people, Tom and Daisy — they smashed up things and creatures and then retreated back into their money or their vast carelessness... (p. 170)**

7

Nick's judgement on the Buchanans could be interpreted as Fitzgerald's judgement on the Roaring Twenties. Six months after the publication of *The Great Gatsby,* he wrote in a letter to Marya Mannes: 'The young

people in America are...brave, shallow, cynical, impatient, turbulent and empty. I like them not...America is so decadent that its brilliant children are damned almost before they are born.'

---

8 **...a fresh, green breast of the new world. Its vanished trees...had once pandered in whispers to the last and greatest of all human dreams... (p. 171)**

Immediately before this reference, Nick was imagining how the Dutch sailors felt when they first arrived in America and saw land. By juxtaposing the green breast and the green light, Fitzgerald makes the green light a symbol of the American Dream, rooted in the past, but forever out of reach. Those who pursue it do so at the expense of the values of a caring society. Those who seem to have achieved it are living in a moral vacuum that destroys any hope of happiness.

---

9 **Gatsby believed in the green light, the orgastic future that year by year recedes before us. (p. 171)**

This paradoxical reference suggests that the light represented the orgasm, the climax of sexual excitement. The 'orgastic future' is the intensity of experience, the dream of fulfilment, towards which all Americans are yearning, but the hope of actually achieving the dream diminishes as each year passes. The ideal future can never be more than an aspiration that actually backs away from us as we reach out for it.

---

10 **So we beat on, boats against the current, borne back cease-lessly into the past. (p. 172)**

Just as a boat which struggles to make progress against too powerful a current is inexorably taken backwards, so Americans pursue their dream of an ideal future, but, in reality, this dream is a hope of recovering the past. Paradoxically, Nick is aware that the dream is not achievable, but that knowledge does not prevent him from striving towards it. The final message of the book is that, as they were promised in the Declaration of Independence, Americans mistakenly pursue happiness by running faster, stretching out their arms further, rowing their boats uselessly against the current, only to find that, like Nick, they must go back to their past.

Taking it further

Websites

- **www.sc.edu/fitzgerald** The University of South Carolina's Scott Fitzgerald centenary webpage contains much useful information. It allows you to hear Fitzgerald reading John Keats' 'Ode to a Nightingale' and watch a brief film clip of Fitzgerald in the 1920s. It also contains a short story by Fitzgerald ('Winter Dreams') with a similar theme to *The Great Gatsby*, and Francis Cugat's original dust jacket illustration for *The Great Gatsby*. There is also a range of essays and articles available.

- **http://faculty.pittstate.edu/~knichols/jazzage.html** Another useful link for context is Pittsburg State University's fascinating website about the Jazz Age.

- **http://webtech.kennesaw.edu/jcheek3/roaring_twenties.htm** Jerrie S. Cheek at Kennesaw State University has published a list of useful online links to information about the USA in the Roaring Twenties.

- **www.bartleby.com/201/1.html** The full text of T. S. Eliot's *The Waste Land*, published just four years before *The Great Gatsby*, is not only useful for context but also for close comparison with Fitzgerald's novel.

- **www.youtube.com/watch?v=3svvCj4yhYc&feature=related** This page on YouTube contains lively and varied video footage of 1920s flappers, accompanied by 1920s music.

More websites are listed online.

Films

1974: directed by Jack Clayton and starring Robert Redford and Mia Farrow, is lovely to watch after you have studied the book and formed your own opinion. You need to beware as it deviates significantly from the book.

2000: made for the BBC and directed by Robert Markowitz. Stars Toby Stephens and Mira Sorvino, makes an interesting contrast with the previous film, but it also makes significant changes so should be watched with caution.

Biographies

- Turnbull, Andrew (1967) *Scott Fitzgerald,* The Bodley Head
  — This is a very readable biography, written by a man who knew Scott Fitzgerald quite well.

Criticism

- Bruccoli, Matthew J. (2000) *F. Scott Fitzgerald's 'The Great Gatsby': A Literary Reference,* Carroll and Graf Publishers
  — This is a vast collection of all the research Bruccoli has collected for his studies of Fitzgerald and his most famous novel. It illuminates the text and provides fascinating background.

- Bruccoli, Matthew J. (ed.) *New Essays on 'The Great Gatsby',* CUP
  — A useful collection of essays offering different interpretations of this novel.

- Mizener, Arthur (ed.) (1963) *F. Scott Fitzgerald: A Collection of Critical Essays,* Twentieth Century Views, Spectrum
  — Another useful collection of differing views about Fitzgerald's work, including *The Great Gatsby.*